Families and work in the twenty-first century

Shirley Dex

JR
JOSEPH
ROWNTREE
FOUNDATION

The **Joseph Rowntree Foundation** has supported this project as part of its
programme of research and innovative development projects, which it hopes
will be of value to policy makers, practitioners and service users. The facts
presented and views expressed in this report are, however, those of the author
and not necessarily those of the Foundation.

Joseph Rowntree Foundation
The Homestead
40 Water End
York YO30 6WP
Website: www.jrf.org.uk

First published 2003 by the Joseph Rowntree Foundation
Published in association with The Policy Press (www.policypress.org.uk)

ISBN: 1 85935 095 X (paperback)
          1 85935 096 8 (pdf: available at www.jrf.org.uk)

A CIP catalogue record for this report is available from the British Library.
Designed by Adkins Design
Printed by Fretwells Ltd

Contents ∎

Preface ■

In the 1990s there was growing concern about the changing nature of both work and family life. Paid work had changed from a predominance of full-time permanent jobs held mostly by men, to a varied mixture of full-time and non-standard forms of employment contracts held by both men and women. Industrial restructuring resulted from increased competition and technological change. Many households were experiencing one or more of: job insecurity, low pay, part-time jobs, long working hours, or severe work-related stress.

In addition to labour market restructuring, there had also been substantial changes in the nature of family relationships. Cohabitation before marriage had increased, as had marital breakdown, lone parent families, out-sourcing of child care, responsibilities of caring for older relatives, and the number of women with independent incomes.

By the end of the twentieth century, the way families related to the labour market and paid work under these changing conditions was under scrutiny. Government policy and consultation documents of the time clearly agreed that vital issues were being raised and needed discussion. Both the availability of paid work, which enables families to be independent, and the stability of family life are important foundations to most people's lives. We need to know how one affects the other, and whether there are virtuous as well as vicious circles of interactions between the two.

A programme of research was launched in late 1997 by the Joseph Rowntree Foundation to examine a number of important themes:

- the effects of work on family life;
- the employer's perspective on work–family relations and social responsibility;
- the relationship of work and family to community resources.

This was an important and innovative step on the part of the Joseph Rowntree Foundation, for which it is to be congratulated. In total, 19 projects were funded to cover these three themes. The programme aimed to contribute to the understanding of these important issues, identify good practice in employment, and explore the nature of genuine family-friendly employment.

The calls for submissions to this research programme outlined broad areas of interest. The research needs had been charted before the programme started, via a literature review [Dex (ed.), 1999]. The projects funded were selective, in that they relied on quality submissions coming forward on the topics of interest. However, in addition, there was a clear strategy to avoid duplication of research funded under existing research programmes: for example, the

ESRC's Future of Work Programme, the DfEE (later DfES) and Joseph Rowntree Foundation's other research programmes. For these reasons, this programme did not fund any new work on homeworking, long hours of work, or no-earner families, and was selective about its funding of research on child care and the child-care workforce. Obviously, the omission from this programme of focused work on these topics is not an indication that they are unimportant, but merely indicates that they were already being covered elsewhere. Inevitably with this kind of programme, just as there was selection in the projects undertaken, there will have been selection in the issues that were raised and the extent to which current policy was addressed.

It is now time to assess what has been learnt. The benefit of a programme of research is that advances to our understanding and lessons can be learnt which cut across the individual projects and their specific briefs. Of the 19 projects funded under this programme, almost all were completed at the time of writing this overview. This provided the opportunity to take a step back from the individual project findings, to ask more general questions and to synthesise the messages that have emerged on issues the programme addressed.

The authors of the separate reports may not all agree with points I have drawn from their research. In fact, we had some lively debates along the way in the Advisory Groups and at the preliminary draft stages of some reports. I have not been trying to re-analyse their data. The selections I have made and the emphases I have given in this overview to findings from separate projects are clearly my own personal views, and should not be attributed to those who carried out the research. But, in my own defence, I unlike they have had the benefit of involvement in the whole programme of research in reaching my conclusions. I have been able to put findings from separate projects alongside each other, to show similarities, differences and qualifications. I certainly wanted to stand back and see something of the wood from the trees.

One thing that was not anticipated at the outset to this research programme was the pace of change that would be set by the Labour government which came to power in 1997. An enormous number of new initiatives and new legislation have been enacted since 1998 (see Box 1). The changes have occurred mid-project for many studies, and this has caused the researchers a number of challenges. It was too early to assess the effects of legislative changes for employees, families or employers. But researchers were not investigating a steady state. Some of the research findings are comments on a period of enormous change – especially for employers. It may be the case that research always faces some change and transition, as the world cannot be held still. But the scale of policy change over this period has been unusual, and is probably not yet finished.

It is not the case that the findings from these various projects are redundant or obsolete because the policy framework changed so much. But it is necessary to bear the nature of this period of transition in mind when discussing the implications for policy of the programme's findings. In some cases, the timing was such that it was possible to feed individual project findings into government consultations on particular topics. This occurred particularly in the consultations around Parental Leave and the Work and Parents Taskforce.

Box 1: **Summary of the policy and legislative developments since 1997 relevant to work and family life**

Working Time Directive
This European directive laying down a maximum of 48 hours (averaged over 17, 26 or even 52 weeks) came into force in October 1998. The directive also confers a right to three weeks paid annual leave, rising to four in November 1999, and minimum weekly rest periods.

The Part-Time Work Directive
This was agreed in December 1997, and came into force by July 2000, to ensure that part-time workers received no less favourable treatment than full-time workers in terms of pay, holidays, public holidays, access to occupational pension schemes, sick pay, maternity/parental leave and training.

National Child Care Strategy
A framework and consultation on child-care provision in Britain (DfEE, 1998). Also overlapping the *Sure Start* programme, announced in 1998, with gradual introduction of increased child-care and early-education places – alongside health and family support – initially particularly for children from disadvantaged areas, but gradually extending to all 3- to 4-year-olds.

National Strategy for Carers
A framework and consultation document on provisions for the needs of those caring for older adults in Britain (DH, 1999).

Parental Leave Directive
The Employment Relations Act 1999 gave working parents the right to take unpaid leave of 13 weeks for each child born after 15 December 1999, up to the child's fifth birthday, implementing the Parental Leave Directive. An extension to these arrangements was announced on the 25th April 2001 in a DTI Press Release, extending the time off from 13 to 18 weeks for parents of disabled children, and extending the basic arrangements to all children who were under five at 15 December 1999.

Time-off for dependants
The Employment Relations Act 1999 gave working parents the right to take a reasonable amount of time off work to deal with uncertain, unexpected or sudden emergencies involving people who depend on them, and to make any necessary longer-term arrangements.

Work–life Balance: Changing Patterns in a Changing World (DfEE, 2000)
This launched an initiative to widen the extent of flexible working arrangements in Britain (DfEE, 2000), including the Work–Life Balance Challenge Fund, offering help to employers to introduce flexible working arrangements.

> **Work and Parents: Competitiveness and Choice. A Green Paper (DTI, 2000)**
> The Work and Parents Taskforce (2001), set up by the Department of Trade and Industry to consider the possibility of new light-touch legislation giving employees a right to request flexible working arrangements. The outcome is embedded in the Employment Act 2001. From April 2003, parents of a child under six have the right to request flexible working arrangements from their employer, who has a duty to give their request serious consideration.
>
> **Employment Act (2001)**
> The *2001 Budget* announced changes now embedded in the Employment Act (2001)
>
> - extension of *maternity leave* – from 18 to 26 weeks from April 2003;
> - increases in *maternity pay;*
> - paid *adoption leave* from 2003;
> - right to two weeks paid *paternity leave* from 2003.

The rest of this overview is organised under four thematic headings, which begin with the relationships between families and macro-level labour markets (Chapter 1: Families and labour markets). This is followed by a chapter on relationships to organisations (Chapter 2: Flexibility and the changing organisation of work). The micro-level experiences of families and their members are then considered (Chapter 3: The effects of paid work on family life). The opportunities for partnerships between these various agents are discussed in Chapter 4 (Partnerships and support), followed by some general conclusions (Chapter 5: Final conclusions).

The Appendix contains a full list of the projects funded under the Work and Family Life programme, with details about their samples and methods, and information on how to obtain published reports and *Findings* summaries. This has been included to give the reader a full picture of the work within the programme. It also identifies some JRF-funded research from outside the programme which has been drawn on for this report.

I have very much enjoyed my association with this programme of research and welcomed this opportunity to draw attention to some of its important findings.

Shirley Dex

Acknowledgements ■

A number of people contributed to this overview of the Work and Family Life Programme. Barbara Ballard, Ceridwen Roberts and Suzan Lewis all provided useful and critical feedback about the document in draft and have improved it by their comments. Clearly this overview rests on the research work of the separate projects.

I am grateful to the Joseph Rowntree Foundation for funding my work on this overview, and for giving me time and space to reflect on what has been learnt, as well as for funding the programme. It has been an interesting and rewarding experience. I am especially grateful to Barbara Ballard, who has worked hard and conscientiously to help this programme of research, and its individual projects, reach successful and relevant conclusions. It has been a very happy and informative experience to work alongside Barbara, with her considerable skill as a research manager.

The researchers on the individual projects are all to be thanked for their work. Also the many Advisory Group members, who played a useful and valuable role in each project, widening horizons and bringing relevance – and sometimes challenge – to project teams.

1 Families and labour markets

Labour markets and families have been subject to enormous changes over the second half of the twentieth century. There have been major changes in women's education and mothers' participation in the labour force. Part-time employment among women has grown, and men's work and labour market institutions have changed. In the labour market, the further decline of agriculture and of manufacturing jobs held by men, together with the growth of service jobs – taken up by women, have resulted in a very different structure of employment.

Since the 1980s, Britain has also experienced deregulation in its labour markets, with an associated decline in trade union membership and activity. Trade unions had been blamed for the failure of British industry to carry out necessary restructuring. There are now debates about the future of work in Britain, in particular about whether Britain's economic health necessitates accepting deregulated un-unionised low paid jobs – the low road to success – or whether the future must be about upgrading skills and knowledge.

Families and family life have been caught up in these changes. It is against this background that the Joseph Rowntree's Programme of Research on Work and Family Life was launched.

Over the past half century the growth of 1.5-earner households (one full-time and one part-time wage), although sometimes mistakenly referred to as two-earner households, has been such that this form of family economic activity is now the dominant pattern (Figure 1). Mothers have entered the labour force partly as a result of their own increased educational qualifications, which have generated a desire and an interest in working outside the home. Legislation on equal opportunities and equal pay for women have also changed the climate in which mothers are employed. The effects of their own increased qualifications and the new climate have contributed to mothers having much higher potential earnings than in the past. This also makes the 'opportunity cost'[1] of caring for children higher and less attractive, given care also has a low value in society at large.

Mothers have also responded to the decline in men's real wages and the growing insecurity of men's earnings, which started in manufacturing sector male jobs and agriculture, but in the 1990s clearly spread to professionals and managerial occupations. The desire of many families to have 1.5 or two earners is linked to reducing the risks attached to this growing threat to men's job security and to the high costs of housing.

---

1 Opportunity cost is the amount that you could be earning, or the amount you forgo in the alternative best activity. If other opportunities would pay more per hour, the opportunity cost of one hour goes up. If you have to forgo more lucrative opportunities to care for your own children, then it becomes relatively less attractive. If you have no alternative earning options, the opportunity cost would be zero. Any changes in these relative prices/costs will affect (some) people's decisions at the margin.

Figure 1: **Couples with dependant children, by number of earners, Great Britain[1]**

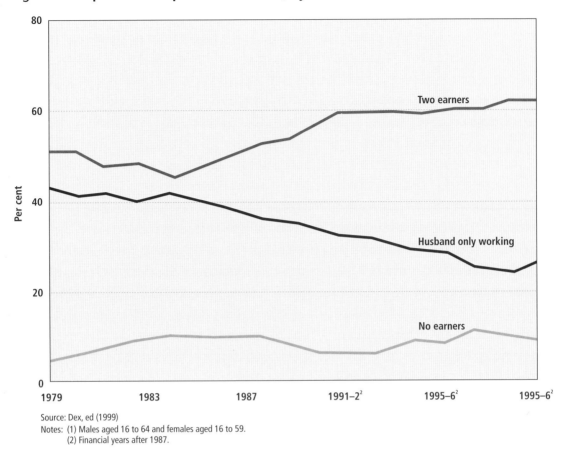

Source: Dex, ed (1999)
Notes: (1) Males aged 16 to 64 and females aged 16 to 59.
       (2) Financial years after 1987.

The increases in mothers' employment have led to them becoming part of the aggregate labour supply, and brought them into new and more public relationships with employers. It is well documented that women have taken jobs in particular segments of the labour market, often working mainly with other women in sex-segregated enclaves.

As well as the growth in part-time work, employment outside of the 'normal' working hours of 9 to 5 during weekdays has also increased. This is associated with the longer hours of highly qualified professionals and managers, men more than women. In part, it represents the growth in services that need to be offered to those who could not otherwise make use of their earnings. Our economic goal of full employment requires people to be able to spend, in order for jobs to be created in producing goods and services. Some of the newest consumers, women, now have additional spending power as a result of their participation in the labour force, but can only spend their earnings if they can shop or buy services when they are not at work. Producers of services, who want women (and men) to be able to spend, need to make sure they can do so outside of normal working hours. This drives forward the '24/7' society, where goods and services are available all day, every day.

Women and mothers now fill many of the paid caring jobs in the health service, child-care professions, retail and social services, instead of doing some of these jobs without pay at home – as they have done in the past. Care needs have increased at both ends of the age spectrum. Having two employed parents means that pre-school children, and school-aged children to a lesser extent, need non-parental care for at least part of each day. Hence the demand for paid child-care has been increasing. People are living much longer and expectations about the state of health that people have a right to expect have risen. Yet many women, the traditional carers, are now in the labour market and not as available to give unpaid care. The National Health Service and Social Services clearly are struggling to cope with these new demands and have insufficient resources. A complex social system has been disturbed and we have yet to see if it can settle down to a new equilibrium.

We are currently in a state of transition, as a mixture of public- and private-sector care initiatives respond – somewhat belatedly in the UK – to changes in parents' behaviour and a lengthening lifespan. The government's National Child Care Strategy and the linked programme Sure Start aimed to ensure that good quality, affordable child care was available for children aged 0–14 in every neighbourhood (especially disadvantaged neighbourhoods in the case of Sure Start). Since 1998 these programmes have made some impact, although new private sector child-care businesses have grown up to offer services to the new workforce. After-school provision, which was particularly sparse, is increasing. Are these provisions adequate, affordable and accessible? The research studies in this programme have some messages on these issues, mostly from detailed qualitative interviews with parents and carers. However, there was never an intention to carry out an exhaustive programme of research on the care workforce in this Work and Family Life Programme.

Against this background of substantial change, this programme has investigated a number of topics at the interface between parents and labour markets. There are new findings on the following topics:

- the extent of parents' (both mothers' and fathers') involvement in atypical working hours;
- in-depth understanding of parents' motivations for working;
- mothers who opt to be self-employed;
- the nature and sustainability of the childminder labour force;
- child-care issues relating to working atypical hours;
- the importance for parents of the geography and coordination of child-care provision;
- work and care issues for the self-employed labour force;
- labour market issues relating to caring for older adults.

Parents' participation in the labour market

Fifty-nine per cent of women aged 16–59 with dependent children were in employment in 1991 (21 per cent in full-time and 37 per cent in part-time employment). In comparison, there were 61 per cent in 1996 (23 per cent full-time and 38 per cent part-time) and 65 per cent in 2001 (26 per cent full-time and 39 per cent part-time). The group showing the largest increases was those women with a youngest dependent child aged 0–4, increasing from 43 per cent in 1991 (14 per cent full-time and 29 per cent part-time) to 54 per cent in 2001 (18 per cent full-time and 36 per cent part-time) (*Labour Market Trends*, 2002).

Regular data on fathers' employment status are not routinely available. The most recent, specially commissioned, analysis of fathers' employment shows little change over the 1990s. Of fathers in couples with a youngest child aged 0–4, 91 per cent were in employment in 1990, compared with 89 per cent in 1997. A similar level of change is evident for fathers of children in other age groups (Holtermann et al., 1999).

Working atypical hours has become commonplace for many parents. A survey of such activity in 2001 was one of the research projects in this programme. A large-scale representative sample of parents with at least one child between the ages of 2 and 16 (La Valle et al., 2002) found:

- Twenty-one per cent of mothers and 41 per cent of fathers worked early mornings, between 6 and 8.30 am at least several times a week.
- One-quarter of mothers and 45 per cent of fathers worked between the hours of 5.30 to 8.30 pm several times a week.
- Fourteen per cent of mothers and 17 per cent of fathers worked evenings or nights (after 8.30 pm) several times a week.
- Thirty-eight per cent of mothers and 54 per cent of fathers worked at least one Saturday a month.
- One-quarter of mothers and just under one-third of fathers worked once a month or more on Sundays.
- Fourteen per cent of mothers and 17 per cent of fathers work at least 2–3 Saturdays *and* Sundays per month.
- Eighteen per cent of mothers and 36 per cent of fathers were required to be on call outside normal working hours.
- One-half of fathers and 13 per cent of mothers regularly worked over 40 hours per week; 30 per cent of fathers and six per cent of mothers worked over 48 hours per week – above the limit of the Working Hours Directive.

Grouping these experiences together under the heading *atypical work*, and picking out those who do this frequently, just over one-half of mothers, 53 per cent (54 per cent of lone mothers), and 79 per cent of fathers frequently worked atypical hours. Examining couples' combined working times, it was found that in 43 per cent of cases both parents concurrently worked atypical hours frequently. In a further 36 per cent of couples, only the father worked atypical hours frequently. These figures show that atypical work has become a pervasive pattern of working for British parents at the end of the twentieth century. In the light of these statistics, we may need to reflect on whether it is appropriate to use the term 'normal working hours'.

Self-employed parents were investigated in this programme through large-scale nationally representative surveys of parents (Bell and La Valle, 2003), and through qualitative case studies. The definition of self-employment is not clear-cut, and there are many and increasing nuances in the way the workforce is classified between self-employed, freelance, franchisee, fixed-term contracts and a new legal term – 'worker'. This is one of the features of our changing British labour market. These surveys, as is common, used parents' self-definitions of whether they were self-employed. Mothers and fathers in couples are more likely than the populations of employed women and men in general to be self-employed, partly because the self-employed tend to be older and are not recent entrants to the labour market. In 1999–2001, eight per cent of mothers and 16 per cent of fathers with a child under 14 were self-employed. There were notable differences in behaviour and motivation between self-employed mothers and fathers who had employees (constituting one quarter of self-employed parents) and those who were self-employed without employees.

Self-employed parents, and especially those with employees, worked much longer hours than employee parents (Bell and La Valle, 2003).

- Twenty-five per cent of self-employed mothers and 71 per cent of self-employed fathers with employees worked more than 45 hours per week;
- 14 per cent of self-employed mothers and 52 per cent of self-employed fathers without employees worked more than 45 hours per week, compared with five per cent of employee mothers and 42 per cent of employee fathers.

The self-employed mothers and fathers were also far more likely to work on Saturdays, Sundays and from home than employees: and those self-employed with employees more so than those without employees.

One group of mothers who are not expected to be in the workforce are mothers of disabled children. This assumption among service providers and employers makes this group into an invisible population in the workforce and the community, as well as in the work–family literature, as an earlier Joseph Rowntree Foundation study of this group pointed out (Kagan et al., 1998). Some of their needs are the same as other mothers in the workforce, and some are different, as described in the rest of this report.

Reasons for working

Parents' reasons for working have been regularly investigated through large-scale official surveys. In the case of mothers, this has led to statistics being cited about how many mothers work to pay for necessities. In one of the earliest surveys in 1980, for example The Women and Employment Survey (Martin and Roberts, 1984), the fact that 30 per cent of employed married women (38 per cent of full-timers and 24 per cent of part-timers) said they worked to pay for necessities served to challenge the earlier myths that married women worked mainly for non-essentials – 'pin money' (Martin and Roberts, 1984). Subsequent statistics have reinforced this view that the single most important reason for mothers working is to earn money. Discussion has taken place in the past about the relative importance to mothers of the job, versus the emphasis placed on getting suitable child-care, in their decision to work. The studies in this programme have some light to throw on this complex issue.

There are of course different types of work, different hours of work and different times of day that work can be carried out. In this programme, some of the reasons underpinning these varying choices about work have been examined – both through surveys and by qualitative research methods. The reasons for working at atypical times varied between mothers and fathers. Survey findings (La Valle et al., 2002) found:

- 75 per cent of mothers who worked at atypical times said this was a requirement of the job rather than a choice;
- the majority of mothers also said they would prefer to work different hours;
- 24 per cent of mothers said they worked atypical hours because it was easier for child-care arrangements, or because partners could look after the children (29 per cent of partnered mothers);
- eight per cent of lone mothers working atypical hours cited the availability of non-resident fathers as their reason for working atypical hours.

There was a tendency for mothers in lower socio-economic groups to give the fact that their partner would care for the children as the reason. But in other ways there was relatively little variation in the responses of mothers from different socio-economic groups.

Self-employed mothers were highly likely to be motivated to be self-employed for child-care reasons, particularly those without employees. The dominance of child care in the decision for mothers to become self-employed was uncovered by this programme's research (Bell and La Valle, 2003; Baines et al., forthcoming 2003). However, qualitative research on parents' decisions to work brought out the complex array of issues that have to be addressed simultaneously if both parents have jobs (La Valle et al., 2002).

Parents' attitudes towards working and towards mothers working were relevant, as were their aspirations, the behaviour of different family members, labour market opportunities and child-care provision. The researchers identified three main and distinct objectives underpinning the decision to work atypical hours. First, families had to balance work with looking after and spending time with children. This issue sometimes meant career ambitions were described as 'being on hold', especially for women but also for a few men. Projects interviewed more than a few men in different occupations who said they had given up career ambitions, but not the full-time breadwinner role, to give more time to their families (Reynolds et al., 2003; Crompton et al., forthcoming 2003; La Valle et al., 2002; Mauthner et al., 2001). It is not clear from these studies how widespread this feeling of sacrifice is among men. It has gone largely unrecognised in earlier research, with women's sacrifices for their families taking centre-stage.

Second, work enjoyment and ambition were main motivations, especially for those who felt a high degree of identity and value in their work (e.g. nurses and police who worked shifts) (La Valle et al., 2002), even though the atypical hours demanded by such jobs made it hard to combine work and family life. Third, financial gain or imperative was a major consideration of those who were doing the only job they could get, whether skilled or unskilled manual jobs and especially in retail. Fathers' atypical work was more linked to financial necessity, job insecurity, career ambitions and long working hours. Mothers who worked atypical hours were more likely to do this as a way of reconciling work and family. However, all three sets of reasons were clearly evaluated by one father:

> *"It's a mix of all those things...if I was looking at a job I would be looking at the hours...but it would have to be the remuneration you have, if you were forced to work awkward hours then how much is that worth to you, that's it at the end of the day is what you've got to think about."*
>
> Father: La Valle et al., 2002

A father's insecure employment was a forceful reason for many mothers to be employed in three rural communities studied (Mauthner et al., 2001). All three communities had suffered declining work opportunities for men, to varying degrees. In some cases this had prompted women to take up part-time jobs; in other cases they took up full-time jobs. It is not quite clear why this difference in response occurred, although it may have been due to the availability of different jobs.

The study of a group of self-employed from disadvantaged backgrounds in the North East found that many men and women became self-employed as their only option for employment (Baines et al., forthcoming 2003). Parents found it was important to have a package of income sources between them, to reduce the risk and vulnerability they felt about household finances. However, self-employment on its own, for those cases studied, was often not a secure or successful way of earning a living. Income support could be far more secure and dependable:

> *"I've never had much money. I wouldn't say that I was well off on benefits because I struggled to feed us and manage every week, but I knew that my rent was paid every week. I knew that my council tax was paid. I didn't have to worry about anything like that."*
>
> Self-employed lone mother: Baines et al., forthcoming 2003

The child-care labour force

The increasing participation of mothers in the labour force has generated an increase in children being cared for by non-parental child-carers. Parents' ways of combining work and child care are discussed more extensively in Chapter 4, as an example of partnership between parents and other carers. Here we focus on the labour-market issues generated by this increase in out-sourced child care.

One of the key questions that is being asked about the child-care workforce is whether it can expand in quantity, quality and flexibility to meet the new demands from two-earner and other households, as well as meeting government targets. The child-care workforce has clearly expanded, alongside the expansion of provision. Since this workforce is varied in nature and characteristics by type of child-care provision, a detailed study of each component is necessary to get a better understanding of the whole workforce. There is a need to understand, for each group, why they are doing the jobs they are doing, how long they stay and what attracted them to it in the first place. This understanding is necessary for an evaluation of whether the workforce can be retained and trained, and whether this workforce can be expanded or recruited.

This programme contributed two studies of the child-care workforce to help address the larger issues. One study covered the childminders' labour market (Mooney et al., 2001). The provision of child care at atypical times of day was examined in the other study (Statham and Mooney, 2003). These studies have added valuable insights into the issues relating to size, quality and flexibility of the national child-care workforce. Other components of the bigger picture are being filled in by research by the DfES, the government department that holds the responsibility for the National Child Care Strategy (for example, see La Valle et al., 2000; Woodland et al., 2002; DfES, 2001).

Childminders

A key factor in the quantity of childminding is childminders' attitudes towards their job, and whether they see it as a career. Although a substantial number of childminders see their work as a long-term career, the majority see it as one phase in their working life coinciding with having young children of their own (Mooney et al., 2001). One childminder captured the main motivation to childmind:

> *"Childminding is an excellent job for a parent who wishes to stay at home with their own children yet still contribute to the family budget"*
>
> Mooney et al., 2001

These women are also those for whom the rewards of other work outside the home were low. After they had paid for their own substitute child care, taking other jobs was not a viable economic alternative.

Numbers of childminders, according to the DoH/DfES statistics and the members' register of the National Childminders Association (NCMA), had been declining in the 1990s. The programme's investigation of this issue did not provide definite answers to why this was the case. One possible explanation was that there had been some tidying-up of the registers of childminders, deleting those who were no longer working as childminders. But there was no hard evidence that this was part of the explanation. The Children Act of 1989, the National Child Care Strategy and, more recently, the switch of inspection and regulation to OFSTED have all left their mark on the regulation of childminding. The process of registering as a childminder has been made more rigorous and, therefore, more difficult for childminders. Similarly, the standards expected of their home are more regulated and demanding to fulfil, although start-up grants to buy toys and other necessary equipment are now available. Even so, the new regulations may be off-putting to potential childminders.

The temporary nature of this workforce, and the increased regulation and hurdles to becoming a childminder both suggest that this source of child care cannot be expected to expand to help fulfil the government's targets for increases in provision. Other studies have tended to agree (see Rolfe et al., 2003). Innovation is clearly possible, as Statham and Mooney (2003) found. But it is on a very small scale and not always economically viable. Increases in a labour force can often be obtained by raising the wage rates. But again, this route to increasing the workforce, be it childminders or other child-care workers, is unlikely to be easy. There seems to be an overwhelming assumption that any child-care costs need to be paid out of the mother's earnings, and not from the family's total earnings. This means that the mother's decision to work is based on a calculation of the economics of hourly wages minus hourly child-care costs. The viability of child-care provision, therefore, is linked to women's wages in general. If these are low, as many are, then it becomes impossible to raise the price of substitute care. As one childminder said:

"You can't charge too much, because you price yourself out of the market. So you're not earning enough to be fully independent, but at the same time you can't afford to ask for more, because then you'll have no work at all."

Childminder: Mooney et al., 2001

Childminders' morale and motivation are also undermined by one of the same forces that prompted mothers to go into paid work in the first place. Childminders, like mothers who used to stay at home to look after their own children, feel that caring for children, even if it is paid, is not particularly valued by society at large. It can also be lonely, since it is done at home. In comparison, doing other paid jobs has higher status, social interaction – which is valued by women – and, often, higher material rewards and satisfaction.

As far as the quality of care is concerned, there is a delicate balance to maintain. Too much additional regulation or inspection for this group, or forcing them to do training, would be likely to lead to further depletion of the stock of childminders. The study showed that there is no intrinsic opposition to training for this workforce, but the interest in training faces structural constraints. As well as meeting the costs of training, there is the issue of child care for the childminder's own children during training time, and the loss of earnings while training (and disruption to the parents who use this child care). These are not insurmountable problems if resources were available, but they need to be seriously addressed if childminders are to be expected to undergo further training. On the other hand, this programme's study of parents who use childminders found them highly satisfied, failing to voice any concerns about the quality of care (Mooney et al., 2001).

Childminders are a group of the child-care workforce that unusually offer flexibility to parents. There is potential for parents to negotiate the start and finish times for the care in ways that are often not possible with day/nursery care. However, at the same time, work outside of a normal working day is not particularly desirable for childminders, just as it is not for many other workers. Childminders are also often more flexible over school holidays. In this sense, childminders are one of the few groups of the child-care workforce who are addressing the flexibility problems, as Statham and Mooney (2003) noted. Their potential to fill this gap further is likely to be limited by virtue of their numbers being unlikely to expand significantly. Those who work atypical hours are those most likely to seek and benefit from more flexible child care. This was the focus of the other project on the child-care workforce.

Provision at atypical times

As parents are working increasingly outside of the 9 to 5 day, it seemed likely that some of these may wish to access child care at such times. There is a question of whether, and to what extent parents want to have formal child-care available outside of so-called normal working hours? There are the additional questions of whether child-care provision is being and can be provided at such times? Statham and Mooney's (2003) project in this programme set to examine these questions by asking some of the key agents for their views; namely, local authorities responsible for child care (Early Years Development and Childcare Partnerships, EYDCP), national child-care organisations, and some child-care providers. The part of this project that refers to demand for child care at atypical times is discussed in Chapter 4.

On the issue of whether such demand is being met, 70 per cent of the EYDCP agents thought that the demand was being partly met, and 18 per cent thought that it was not being met at all. However, it was clear from surveying providers that a sizeable group, mainly childminders, had made marginal adjustments to their care hours, mostly by extending the end of the day. Flexibility has therefore been increasing. The problems in offering child care in the early morning, late evenings or at weekends fell under four broad headings:

- there was a problem in getting staff, especially existing staff, to work at atypical times of day;
- there were funding problems in providing such services at these times of day and sustainability problems, given the demand is relatively low;
- some felt it was a choice between extending their existing service versus developing new ones;
- problems of meeting regulatory and registration requirements were also anticipated.

Underlying the staffing problem, again, is the low pay and low status attached to child-care work that, given it affects recruitment and retention of day-time staff, may be worse for staff required to work at atypical times. Although this study made suggestions about ways forward, one cannot but conclude that these are fairly formidable problems.

Leverage in the labour market

In these times of skill shortages it might be expected that individuals with certain jobs had leverage in the labour market to get better pay and conditions, or have a greater degree of choice. The study of working at atypical times confirmed this expectation to some extent (La Valle et al., 2002). In occupations like teaching and nursing, the higher level of demand meant that some parents had considerable choice about types of jobs and working arrangements. Similarly, high qualifications and skill levels enhanced choice. Low skill-levels, or highly specialised work, particularly in declining industries and in the three rural areas included in one study (Mauthner et al., 2001), were both associated with limited choice. Adding health problems or disability into the picture also reduced choice and parents' bargaining position. Those with less choice, not surprisingly, were those who expressed most concern about job security, and identified keeping a job as the main priority.

Mothers with low skill levels appeared to have more choice than low skilled fathers. Some mothers had moved out of factory work into care jobs, which they found both more rewarding and with working hours that suited their family needs better. Men did not appear to have the same choices and felt the burden of being the breadwinner (La Valle et al., 2002; Reynolds et al., 2003). On the other hand, those with stronger bargaining positions often felt responsibilities towards the job and a commitment to do extra hours when required. The greater choice of these better-placed workers was, in practice, eroded by an unwillingness to make use of it.

A study of employers' relocations also showed that highly qualified employees could be forced to move area by their employer, with little thought being given to the family consequences (Green and Canny, 2003). Interestingly, employees at lower levels of skill resisted such moves if they arose, and were thought by employers to be immoveable, or possibly not worth the costs of moving. Workers at low skill levels were more likely to give priority to family life in their decision-making, women especially, but men also.

The idea canvassed by sociologists (Beck, 1992), that risk has been shifted away from employers and towards employees, was evident in many examples across the studies, but mainly among fathers rather than mothers. The absence of trade unions, the growth of individualised employment contracts and individual bargaining have all left employees more exposed, more vulnerable and less likely to contest their conditions of work. There were many examples, among both highly skilled and less skilled employees, of thinking that the employer held all the cards if they wanted career progression or job security (Mauthner et al., 2001; Green and Canny, 2003). The employer's power came out most strongly when they wanted to move employees from one location to another. However, employers were finding greater resistance to relocate among employees in dual earner couples. The risk of losing a job by refusing to relocate may, at some point, be balanced and outweighed by the increased risk and dissatisfaction of a spouse having to give up a job if the whole family move.

The pay economy

The studies in this programme have shown families being involved across the range of labour markets, the paid formal economy and particularly heavily involved in the growing 24/7 sector. But underpinning the formal paid contracts are a set of informal relationships – without which the paid economy would be unable to function. More of these are to be seen in later chapters. Where levels of working hours can be kept in the reasonable range, the 1.5 earner strategy for reducing risk seems to work reasonably well as a provider of independence and support for families. Those who are living most on the edge of financial viability are the self-employed who have started businesses in order to avoid unemployment and lone parents who are employed. This programme did not study the unemployed no-earner households, the 'time-rich work-poor families', since it focused on families who have a relationship with the labour market. However, there were some families who had made the transition to self-employment from state benefit, who described the enormous sense of risk they felt from leaving the relative security of the benefit system. It is clear from the illustrations of 1.5 earner families in this programme that, in this new economy of increased risk, the 1.5 earner household seems to be a reasonably successful family strategy. However, where there were above-average numbers of children, combining paid work and family for mothers seemed to pose greater problems, to the extent that some mothers felt it to be impossible (Skinner, 2003).

2 Flexibility and the changing organisation of work

Balancing the demands of paid work and care has become an important policy topic in most industrialised countries since women entered the labour force in large numbers. Some would say it is a key workplace issue of our time. The growth of 1.5 earner families, increasing family breakdown, increasing pressures and intensity at work have been linked to feelings of pressured lives. These feelings have their workplace outcomes in increasing levels of sickness, turnover, stress and absence from work. Business leaders and government are regularly noting the large costs involved. The fact that many families, and society more generally, need a better work–life balance is not disputed. How to obtain this goal is more of a challenge. A better work–life balance is one of the factors politicians have identified to help address increasing work-related stress and ill health, and possibly in due course, the rising costs of care for older people. It is important to know whether or not this makes business sense across different sizes and sectors of business. This programme was able to look at this issue in a number of ways and has generated new findings on several workplace-related issues, including:

- the business case for flexible working arrangements;
- awareness of and take-up issues relating to flexible working arrangements;
- the effects of flexible working on employee commitment;
- the effects on careers of taking up employer offers of flexible working arrangements;
- approaches to flexible working in small and medium-sized enterprises (SMEs);
- the problems employers face in introducing flexible working arrangements;
- the employee's perspectives on flexible working;
- equity issues relating to flexible working arrangements.

The business case

The view that there is a business case for introducing greater flexibility in employees' working arrangements has been put forward by such employers' organisations as Opportunity NOW (previously Opportunity 2000), the government and other interested business parties. It has been claimed that there are productivity, recruitment and retention gains from allowing employees to work more flexibly. In addition, even where there are costs to the new provisions, the potential benefits and savings on, for example, absence, sickness and staff turnover may make it beneficial to make some changes. Evidence has been mounting for this viewpoint, although necessarily it has accumulated in a somewhat piecemeal fashion.

A review of case studies of organisations that had introduced some kind of flexible working arrangements up to 1998 found that many had registered benefits from comparing performance measures before and after its introduction (Dex and Scheibl, 1999; Bevan et al.,

1999). Through the government's Work–Life Balance Challenge Fund, which started in 2000, there may, in due course, be several hundred further cases of employers who demonstrably have also benefited from introducing flexible working arrangements.

Until the start of this programme, an extensive investigation of the case for there being benefits of flexible working for a wide range of industries and workplaces had foundered on the lack of suitable data. Case studies of individual workplaces where flexibility has been introduced, even if performance were measured carefully before and after, still leave the possibility that such workplaces are not typical: they could be organisations that are more likely to benefit by using flexible working arrangements. A large-scale study of a nationally representative sample of organisations, some of which have flexibility while other do not, would be able to control for other differences between the organisations and measure whether flexibility adds to performance, after controlling for these differences. Such a dataset became available in 1998 in Britain (Airy et al., 1999): The Workplace Employee Relations Survey data (WERS98).

WERS98 is a nationally representative sample of British workplaces collected by the DTI. It provided a unique opportunity for this programme to examine the potential performance benefits from flexibility across a wide range of workplaces. Ideally, of course, a stronger case would be made if longitudinal data were available for a nationally representative sample survey of workplaces. But such data are very expensive to collect and, as many cases drop out over time, it is difficult to get good quality data. Nonetheless, the WERS98 data, collected at only one point in time, provided a very valuable opportunity to examine this issue. Given that the WERS98 data included a large amount of other information about the workplaces that it surveyed, it was possible to control for a very large range of workplace characteristics in assessing whether flexible working arrangements have had beneficial effects on the 'bottom line' of business.

This programme's analysis of WERS98 data found that improvements in performance were associated with flexible working arrangements, after controlling for a wide range of other influences on performance (Dex and Smith, 2002). However, the picture is complex. Out of the measures examined, financial performance, labour productivity, quality of product or service, sales, staff turnover and absence, some flexible arrangements were associated with certain business performance measures, but not with others. For example, there was a staff-turnover of 3–4 per cent less per year where there was either flexitime working, job-share arrangements, help with child care or support for working at or from home during normal working hours. Some flexible working arrangements had no statistical associations with performance. There were a few cases where flexible working was associated with lower performance. But the message overall from the results was that performance benefits were associated with flexible working arrangements.

Several case studies of smaller businesses, carried out for another research project, illustrated how the flexibility might produce business benefits (Dex and Scheibl, 2002). The smaller businesses that had embraced flexible working arrangements and had made flexibility integral to their business and culture had both good performance and low staff turnover. The viewpoints of the managing director, the factory manager and an employee all told the same story:

"Our business priority is to encourage staff to develop...It is central to our approach that workers can come to us and ask – we will listen and accommodate their needs when we can...We just get the feeling it is working so well. Profits are up and we can afford to increase pay. We all get flexibility, for example, to go and see a school teacher, or go and do extra shopping. The staff come in extra time to make up if necessary."

Managing director: Dex and Scheibl, 2002

"We like to be able to give the staff what they want knowing that we will get it back. We get back what we give them in loyalty and effort. We have an open phone policy to make sure that all teams can get cover."

Factory manager: Dex and Scheibl, 2002

"If we are busy we pay them back. Because they are so good to you – you want to be good to them and show our commitment. I do not think anyone would abuse it [the system of flexibility]."

Employee: Dex and Scheibl, 2002

The study mentioned earlier of mothers of disabled children repeated these findings. Where these employees were given flexibility, they went out of their way to reciprocate with loyalty and commitment (Kagan et al., 1998).

Access and awareness

In the case study research within organisations there was no widespread evidence of selected groups of employees being entitled to policies offering flexible working, with others failing to have access. However, where formal policies were absent, groups of workers did experience different degrees of informal access to flexible working arrangements, although expectations about the type of work and how it needed to be organised played a large role (Dex and Scheibl, 2002). Studies did not find any examples of policies where women (or men) had access to company policies and the other gender did not. Employers did not expect mothers of disabled children to work, so there were no focused provisions for this group (Kagan et al., 1998). Generally, studies did not find gender differences in the use of the policies, after taking into account the gender and age breakdowns of the workforce. However, line-managers did exercise discretion over employees' access to flexibility (Bond et al., 2002; Yeandle et al., 2002; Phillips et al., 2002). Eligibility could and did vary by work group. Given the tendency for many work groups to be predominantly female or predominantly male, employees' eligibility could vary indirectly by gender for this reason.

The Workplace Employee Relations Survey and other case studies, and project surveys of employees all revealed a consistent picture about the levels of awareness of employees. However, it cannot be assumed that those who are aware of their employers' policies are the sum total of those who could access flexible working arrangements. Awareness was determined by a mixture of the employee's personal characteristics and circumstances, the constraints of the job, and the value of the employee to their employer.

Being female, a parent of young children, a union member or having had recent training made employee awareness and possibly access to flexibility more likely (Dex and Smith, 2002; Bond et al., 2002). Higher qualified workers and those in higher grade or clerical jobs were also more likely than other workers to perceive they had access to flexible working arrangements (Dex and Smith, 2002; Yeandle et al., 2002; Dex and Scheibl, 2002). However, as well as workers' characteristics helping to explain which employees got offered access to flexible arrangements, some workplaces were more likely than others to offer flexibility. The public sector was far more likely than the private sector to offer access to a wide range of flexible working arrangements (Dex and Smith, 2002; Yeandle et al., 2002). Workplaces with union recognition, large size, more developed and good human resources policies, consultation procedures and active equal opportunities policies were also associated with an increased likelihood of being offered flexibility (Dex and Smith, 2002).

The research on the WERS98 data in this programme offered a rigorous analysis of employees' access to and awareness of flexible working arrangements, by controlling for other potential determinants of employee awareness and access at the same time. The fact that the case-study findings overlapped with the statistical analyses strengthened the conclusions.

Clearly, some workplaces faced operational constraints on the flexible arrangements they could offer (Dex and Scheibl, 2002). However, the fact that workplaces which employ mainly men, and particularly those in traditional craft industries and occupations, were less likely to offer flexible working arrangements suggest that traditional attitudes may be playing a role, as well as operational constraints (Yeandle et al., 2002; Dex and Smith, 2002; Houston and Waumsley, forthcoming 2003). Research on smaller businesses in this programme confirmed that traditional attitudes from some male employers and managers led to an exaggeration of the problems to the production process or service delivery that would result if the business were to adopt flexible working arrangements (Dex and Scheibl, 2002).

Factors increasing awareness

Awareness of employers' policies was generally fairly low and found to vary. It was not uncommon for half or more of employees in a workplace to be unaware that their employer had policies relating to employees' caring responsibilities (Yeandle et al., 2002; Phillips et al., 2002; Houston and Waumsley, forthcoming 2003).

- Those who were likely to benefit were more likely to know about the policies, but even then awareness was far from perfect.
- Where managers and the organisations as a whole put more effort into informing employees about their policies, alongside a favourable workplace culture and methods of implementing flexible working that involved employees, they were far more likely to know about the policies and be appreciative of them (Yeandle et al., 2002).

- Awareness in the financial services sector was found to be greater where policies involved paid leave, compared with those offering unpaid leave (Bond et al., 2002).
- Awareness was lowest for provisions that had only recently become statutory and were not yet in the Staff Handbook (Bond et al., 2002).
- Employees also showed greater levels of awareness in unionised workplaces (Bond et al., 2002).
- Smaller organisations often did not have the formal policies, but employees in these smaller organisations were often well aware of the informal practices that might be available to them (Dex and Scheibl, 2002)

.

Line managers' awareness

In addition to employees failing to be aware, there was evidence that line managers were similarly unaware of their organisation's policies in both the private and public sectors (Phillips et al., 2002; Yeandle et al., 2002; Bond et al., 2002). Line managers were better informed in unionised workplaces, where policies were formalised and where they had received training (Bond et al., 2002). There was a tendency for line managers to direct employees to take up policies they were familiar with, especially where they were inexperienced or unsure about the alternatives or more recent provisions (Phillips et al., 2002; Bond et al., 2002). However, individuals' values had a role in how policies were implemented.

One manager expressed the view that she saw emergency leave as a safety net after an employee's annual leave had been used up on the emergencies (Phillips et al., 2002). Other line managers made fine distinctions between deserving and undeserving cases. For example, an individual might be entitled to paid leave if it was a serious illness they needed time off for, but unpaid leave if it was an accident; paid leave if it was close family, but not otherwise (Yeandle et al., 2002).

Although training can assist in line manager's knowledge about their organisation's policies (Bond et al., 2002; Yeandle et al., 2002), with the best will in the world, there is a limit to how much line managers, and employees can take in about an organisation's policies at induction sessions. Often employees and managers will be given the information at a point when they do not need to know it. Strategies need to be devised, therefore, that allow for these inherent knowledge gaps to be filled, especially in contexts where company policies may change. In the case of line managers, they need to be able to access the information when it is needed. Alternatively, and more flexibly, they need to be given freedom (and training) to decide what to do in individual cases, based on assembling and then evaluating the business case for an employee's request.

Some larger organisations have been experimenting with such approaches and finding they have benefits all round. For employees, there is a need to understand that the organisation and managers are approachable and open to hearing their requests. This is a simpler thing to get across to employees and employers, although there is considerably more work to be done in getting at least employees to believe it.

Take-up

In view of the fact that employee awareness of employer policies was low, and not all employees will want to take the opportunities offered, it is perhaps not surprising that take-up was also low. The WERS survey found that in 25 per cent of workplaces that offered some kind of flexible working, no employees had taken them up. For establishments where there had been some take-up, in two-thirds of these cases, it was only a small proportion of the workforce that had used the provisions (Dex and Smith, 2002). These WERS survey responses are unlikely to be based on precise calculations. The vast majority of the organisations researched as part of this programme did not keep accurate records about take-up of their policies. Nonetheless, it is unlikely that managers' impressions of take-up will be drastically inaccurate. The research projects that surveyed their organisations' employees about take-up found it to be at very low levels (Yeandle et al., 2002; Phillips et al., 2002; Houston and Waumsley, forthcoming 2003).

On the other hand, we might want to consider the reasons for the lack of use of the policies from the employee's point of view. A comparison between retail bank branches, supermarkets and local councils found that employees' use of policies was considerably greater in the councils than in the other organisations (Yeandle et al., 2002). However, the gap in take-up between these organisations was much reduced in the case of the policy that allowed employees to reduce their hours. In general, studies found differences in take-up were likely to be related to a number of factors (Yeandle et al., 2002; Bond et al., 2002; Houston and Waumsley, forthcoming 2003):

- whether the flexibility was paid or involved loss of pay;
- the different income levels of jobs in these organisations – affecting the ability to cope with loss of earnings;
- the different age and lifecycle profiles of the workforce, which affected their need for flexibility;
- how long the policy had been offered, i.e. whether it was relatively new or well established;
- levels of staffing and whether colleagues had to work more as a result;
- workplace cultures influencing whether it was seen to be an acceptable thing to do.

Employees clearly differentiate between the various policy provisions of their organisations. Employees use paid leave options if they are available in preference to unpaid options (Bond et al., 2002). This is a well-known employee preference. In part it was one of the early arguments for introducing policies like emergency leave, in order to stop employees abusing paid sick leave, giving them an option where they could be honest instead of deceitful about the reasons for their absence. Where there are paid and unpaid options for leave sitting alongside each other, there is a tendency and built-in incentive for one to undermine the other. The legislation allowing unpaid days off for family reasons is expected to be of limited benefit in these cases. A single paid option to take leave when necessary is a simpler system, which does not give employees an incentive to shirk or lie.

In hard-pressed under-staffed departments, employees also expressed feelings of guilt and not wanting to let down colleagues as reasons for not taking up the flexible opportunities (Phillips et al., 2002; Yeandle et al., 2002).

> "I've known people come in next to death and have an attitude that, unless I physically can't walk, I'll get into work somehow. You get this mindset that you've got to go in at all costs because of the pressure on other people, and I think because you are dealing with a lot of emotive issues…you'd almost feel responsible if you didn't see them [the service user] today and something happened to them."
>
> Social services manager: Phillips et al., 2002

The case-study work in financial services found that policies were more generous in the context where there was an acceptance of long hours of work and less likelihood, therefore, that employees would seek to use their entitlement either to take leave or reduce their hours (Bond et al., 2002).

The effects of flexible working on employee commitment

The WERS98 survey contains information from both managers and employees – which is unusual. It was thus possible to use the survey to examine whether employees' experiences of work varied according to whether or not they were aware that they were being offered flexible working arrangements. The study found that, after controlling for a wide range of influences on commitment, flexible working arrangements were associated with higher employee commitment (defined as loyalty, pride and sharing the values of the organisation) in private sector workplaces. The case studies of smaller private sector businesses that offered flexibility supported this finding, showing that increased loyalty and commitment were generated as a result of employers agreeing to flexible working arrangements (Dex and Scheibl, 2002). Workers expressed this as direct cause and effect (as quotations cited earlier in this chapter illustrate), even though the statistical analysis on the cross-sectional survey data could only establish statistical associations and not causal links.

In the public sector this relationship was not evident. In some cases, flexible working arrangements were associated with lower employee commitment in the public sector workplaces. This is a puzzle. The assumption at the outset had been that the longer duration and more extensive provision of flexible arrangements in the public sector would be welcomed by employees, and their commitment would be raised. The WERS98 survey did not provide data that could be used to examine this issue further. However, other studies in the programme did focus on public sector organisations and have some suggestions to offer that explain public sector employees' responses.

It may be the case that longer exposure to flexible working in the public sector has allowed staff to take it for granted. Brannen et al.'s (2001) study of young people found that some people choose to work in the public sector because of flexibility, but regard it as a trade-off for lower pay compared with the private sector. Having made this compromise, they may be less inclined to feel more committed, especially in the long term. Other studies in the programme found evidence of window-dressing in some public sector organisations. Although the policies were formal and written, the workplace culture did not always reward or encourage flexibility (Phillips et al., 2002; Yeandle et al., 2002). Also, staff shortages made it difficult for employees to take up provisions that were offered by the employer, knowing it would increase the workload of already hard-pressed colleagues. Feelings of being disloyal were common. However, in a few cases, it was felt that staff had abused the provisions. These experiences could lead other staff to become cynical about the arrangements, as one social services department manager expressed:

> "The Department isn't actually very good at taking the policy to its final conclusion and saying 'Bye bye' to anybody...I think it's demoralising to other people around...I'm a bit cynical sometimes about stuff, especially, I think, as a manager, one of the things is that you feel hurt when people lie to you over their real situation and you remember those...I'd like to see quite stern repercussions for people who abuse it...it does seem a bit toothless at times."
>
> Social services manager: Phillips et al., 2002

These studies suggest that some public sector contexts are not conducive to employees benefiting from the flexibility their employer has offered. Window-dressing, staff shortages, lean staffing policies, no cover for absence and possibly some abuse will reduce the potential benefits from flexibility. Employees will not feel able to take up the provisions where the workplace culture sends a message that they should not do so, or where they feel they will be letting colleagues down. These elements need to be managed more equitably if improved performance and staff appreciation are to be achieved.

Effects on careers

An important issue that is raised by different working arrangements is: how do they affect individuals' careers? This is a particularly important question in the light of the rewards associated with working long hours in some organisations. If working part-time, or more flexible arrangements are seen as a 'mummy track' for women with children and definitely not for those interested in promotion or a career, then it will only help family life at the expense of creating a new set of gender stereotypes to reinforce the old framework of occupational segregation. This is a difficult area to research. One ideally needs organisations that offer flexible working arrangements to employees at all grades of staff. There needs to be some clear career routes in the organisation. Ideally, a longitudinal study is required to follow individuals who either take up or do not take up flexible working arrangements, to compare how they progress through the career hierarchies.

One can shorten the data collection process by asking individuals to recall their career moves within organisations, but one has to be aware of the errors that can creep in to their recall, especially of dates and less salient events over short periods of time. However, one cannot easily get over the problem that organisations can change over the period they are being researched (even by recall methods). Changes to organisations' policies and culture along the way can affect later generations, making it difficult to compare them with earlier ones.

One study in this programme addressed the issue of how accessing career breaks and more flexible options affected longer-term prospects in three types of organisation; two local councils; and two branches of both a retail bank and a supermarket (Crompton et al., forthcoming 2003). Since the supermarket and retail bank branch studied were relatively small-sized workplaces, career advancement for staff involved mobility to the organisation's other sites. This was not welcomed by many female staff, who ruled themselves out of considering promotion for this reason. It also proved difficult, given the sizes of the workforces, and the fact that men do not take up flexible working arrangements to the same extent as women, to make comparisons between men who had and men who had not taken up flexible working. That such comparisons would be highly informative on this question cannot be doubted, but must be left to other research to consider.

The study did find examples of women matched by similar positions and circumstances, who had and had not taken a career break in the retail bank or council. The comparisons found that those who had taken a career break had not risen through the ranks of the retail bank or council grades to the same extent as those who had worked full-time without a break. However, it was not entirely clear whether this was because they were discriminated against, or regarded as less committed workers, or because they had less job experience. The question could not be fully resolved because insufficient time had elapsed up to the point of the interview to see whether, in the fullness of time, and having accumulated years of job experience to compensate for the time of the career break, individuals may have reached the same promotion grades as those who did not have a break. It was not clear, therefore, whether those taking career breaks would have been able to move up through the full spectrum of organisations' career structures but at a slower pace.

It was clear that the retail bank's change of policy had facilitated some mothers' careers, compared with those in earlier generations. It was now possible in the retail bank to have a career break and/ or work part-time and still be considered for promotions. This certainly had not been possible when some of the older women had been at the same stage of their career. In order to work part-time these older women would have had to leave the company. These signs of flexibility and change were welcomed by those who were benefiting, and even by women who had never had such opportunities. Overall, this study's findings offered some encouragement for flexible working – albeit from one small-scale study.

On the other hand, the supermarket championed flexible working among its lower grade staff but there was little by way of career structures to move up. Its managers worked long hours. The policies here appeared to be selective in their operation. Taking up flexible arrangements did not seem practical for managers, given their workload. It was not the case that managers failed to be promoted if they did work flexibly. They did not even consider doing so. However, there was often a reluctant acceptance by managers that long hours were needed to manage responsibly and effectively. This had a spillover effect on staff at lower levels, who did not want to consider promotion because it was associated in their minds with the necessity of working very long hours.

Smaller organisations

Smaller organisations have been thought to offer their employees fewer opportunities to work flexibly than larger organisations. The results from the Workplace Employee Relations Survey supported this expectation. But case study work on smaller organisations disputed this earlier impression of a relationship between size and flexible working arrangements (Dex and Scheibl, 2002). Many smaller organisations were found that did not have any formal policies offering flexible working arrangements to their employees, but which nonetheless allowed individuals who came forward with requests, to change their working arrangements. These research findings suggest that it may well be the wording of survey research questions that has given rise to the impression that small means inflexible. Certainly, small means informal, but this is not the same as inflexible. In practice, a spectrum of approaches to allowing employees to have flexible working arrangements was found in smaller businesses.

At one end was a whole-hearted embrace of flexible working arrangements, making them central to the working arrangements, business plan and culture of the organisation. At the other end of the spectrum was resistance. In the middle was the selective use of flexible arrangements, often as a perk or concession for individuals who asked, and who were regarded as worth retaining as an employee. This middle position of selective and informal provision was evident across a range of small businesses, including ethnic minority family businesses (Basu and Altinay, forthcoming 2003). Family membership was sometimes a lever for obtaining flexible working arrangements in all types of business. Owners' or partners' family members were allowed flexibility in some family businesses or partnerships when other employees were not; often, it was claimed, because they could be trusted.

Small businesses in Britain also have a reputation for being anti-regulation. Managing directors and senior managers of the organisations included in this study expressed some of the same views. They were asked in their interviews about how flexible working arrangements, if they were to adopt them, might affect their business. The problems they anticipated included:

- having no substitutes for certain jobs if employees were on leave or worked part-time;
- fears of losing customers;
- disruption and lower productivity;
- more work for managers;
- problems of inequities and resentment from other employees.

What was very interesting about the problems they anticipated was that other small organisations, similar in their products or type of work, did not find these problems arose when flexible working arrangements were used, or they had resolved them by changes in the organisation of work – often to their benefit.

In addition, employers suggested their employees did not want flexibility. This turned out to be far from the truth. This implies that many of the problems anticipated are the (mis)perceptions of small business owners and managers, and would not necessarily arise in practice. It may be that employers who were opposed to flexible working arrangements would resist any changes. Certainly, attitudes that resisted the use of new technology often went alongside resistance to new working arrangements. But small-business owners were also under severe time pressures, and since introducing and implementing change takes time, this was undoubtedly part of the problem.

One challenge for government policy to face if it wants small organisations to change is that it needs to find them some time. The Work–Life Balance Challenge Fund has gone some way towards providing more time for organisations, in the form of paid consultancy. But the companies had to come forward and apply for this, and the time-scale is short. The small businesses that were resistant to introducing flexible working would be unlikely to come forward, and even those which are more sympathetic might find the time it takes to apply prohibitive. Also, changing the mind-sets in companies takes time.

Certain ways of organising the work can assist the smooth operation of flexible working arrangements in smaller, or even larger organisations (Dex and Scheibl, 2002). For example:

- working in teams that are multi-skilled helps work groups to provide cover;
- having a policy of rotating employees or sending them on sabbaticals in other teams;
- flatter management structures were better than the 'command and control' style of management.

It requires more trust to allow people to work at home, out of sight, but employees can respond very positively to such arrangements. Trust also underpinned the use of flexible working arrangements in ethnic minority family businesses (Basu and Altinay, forthcoming 2003). Using a system of reciprocity, preferably one that is explicit, to allow flexibility for employees who had shown they were good workers was popular in several organisations.

All of these practices were evident in the organisations that were benefiting most from their use of flexible working arrangements. As well as being popular with employees, there were other spillovers benefits to the business from some of these practices. Employees got a broader view of the business and were more involved in it and more supportive of its overall aims. There was a genuine sense of partnership between the employer and employees, the latter being able to offer useful suggestions for operational improvements, as earlier quotations illustrate.

Family and care responsibilities – the employee's perspective

As well as hearing from employers about their arrangements, many projects were also able to examine the employee's perspective in the same workplaces. If it is hoped that flexible working will ease the pressures of work on family life, the test of this will be in employees' accounts. More of the detail of experiences of work and family life are described in Chapter 3. Here we focus only on whether problems of paid work for families with children, or those with responsibilities for caring for older adults, are eased when they have flexible working arrangements.

Business size

Employees in small businesses were the most positive that flexibility at work had beneficial carry over effects to the employee's family and personal life.

> "It is very good here; all of the partners have got children themselves....It is very helpful to have this flexibility. It is hard to think of ways that they could make any improvements because this job cannot be done from home. Nothing at this firm makes coping with work and family life difficult."
>
> Employee: Dex and Scheibl, 2002

More problems of combining paid work and care were expressed by employees in larger organisations, in small businesses resistant to flexibility, and where policies were not always translated into practice. Many parents of young and older children noted that school holidays were a problem for them (Yeandle et al., 2002; Backett-Milburn et al., 2001; Mauthner et al., 2001; Skinner, 2003); few expected the employer to take responsibility for a solution.

As well as satisfied users of flexible working arrangements, studies found examples of employees who would very much like to have access to flexibility, even some who had left their employer because of the lack of flexibility (Dex and Scheibl, 2002; Backett-Milburn et al., 2001). It is likely that current usage under-estimates levels of interest in these sorts of working arrangements. Larger-scale surveys outside the programme have also confirmed that there is substantial demand for flexible working-time arrangements (Hogarth et al., 2001).

Carers of older adults

Policies that ideally suited the needs of employees caring for older adults were seen to differ from those needed for parents caring for children. Caring for older adults was less predictable, more variable, could involve some distance, and was less visible and less accepted in comparison with caring for children (Phillips et al., 2002; Yeandle et al., 2002).

Earlier studies of working carers of older adults found they experienced tiredness (43 per cent), stress and anxiety (50 per cent), and that caring affected their career progression (32 per cent) (Princess Royal Trust, 1995). Many had given up trying to care and do a paid job. The same survey suggested that seven out of ten carers under 50 years and eight out of ten in the 56–60 age group had given up paid work. Of those who had given up work, 47 per cent said they would have carried on working if there had been more flexibility at work. The studies of working carers included in this programme uncovered some of the same problems (Phillips et al., 2002; Yeandle et al., 2002).

Clearly, employers' policies to help working carers of older adults are not well developed. This is a Cinderella policy area in organisations' human resource management, but it should not remain so. Given the demographic trends and the possibilities of needing to work longer to finance pension contributions, developing policies to assist working carers needs to become more of a priority.

Where employees had caring responsibilities for older adults, they tended to use annual leave and time off in lieu to cope with the caring responsibilities when they arose (Phillips et al., 2002). This was the case even where the organisation had more specifically targeted policies to address these needs. This meant that working carers did not always benefit from their organisation's policies. There were likely to be longer-term consequences for employees and the organisation in the cases of severe carer responsibilities, where employees were not getting any rest through using up holiday entitlement on caring responsibilities.

Studies of working carers in this programme found that many employed carers were reluctant to publicise their caring responsibilities at work and to use the specific workplace provisions that were there to help (Phillips et al., 2002; Yeandle et al., 2002). This reluctance to access their organisation's provisions may be due to fears that knowledge about their responsibilities could affect their career prospects. Certainly, there was a widespread belief among carers that they needed to be 'seen to be coping' in the workplace. Lone parents interviewed in Edinburgh expressed the same concerns (Backett-Milburn et al., 2001). The existence of these feelings also indicates that there is long way to go before organisations, and even employees themselves, face up to and are comfortable with the fact that all workers have more than one identity; they are all workers *and* mothers, fathers, sons or daughters.

Few of these carers of older adults accessed the state's provisions (Phillips et al., 2002; Yeandle et al., 2002). While the state resources are being stretched to meet current demands for care services for older people, it is clear that demand is far from being at full capacity. A lot of unpaid work is being carried out by many employed carers, some of whom have demanding paid jobs.

Unsocial hours

Businesses throughout the industrialised world have been facing increased competition in the now global marketplace and 24/7 society. This has increased pressure to be competitive, to keep the costs and wage bill low, to seek out new efficiency gains and to introduce lean production processes that use the minimum of workers. For some employers, one response has been to design jobs so they can be filled by the newer, often lower paid, supply of women's labour. For others, expecting employees to work longer hours and harder has been an implicit strategy in their recruitment and reward systems. In both cases there have been increases in working early mornings, evenings and at weekends. In some cases employees' contracts have specified these new times of working as standard; in some cases employees are paid overtime or special rates; and in other cases employees work beyond their contract hours unpaid in order to get the job done.

This proliferation of working-time arrangements has resulted from the same pressures operating in different product market environments. As mentioned in Chapter 1, a large proportion of parents have got caught up in these trends, and are more likely than other workers to be working non-standard hours and patterns as part of formal paid arrangements. The government's own studies have shown the extent of some forms of 'atypical work'. This programme undertook further survey work to investigate both the detail of how parents combined their working-time schedules and what the effects were on family life (described in Chapter 3).

Fathers have two main reasons for working long hours. One is linked to financial necessity and job insecurity (La Valle et al., 2002). This is clearly the driver for lower income families. The other is career ambition, a motivation that operates higher up the income scale. Working long hours, unpaid and beyond contracted hours, has been a growing expectation in higher qualified occupations for both men and women (Hogarth et al., 2000; Dex and Scheibl, 2002). Mothers' reasons for working at atypical times were often linked to the desire to balance work and family life, and were seen, therefore, as part of the solution to combining work and family for mothers. However, a smaller proportion of mothers worked long hours for the same reasons as men.

Clearly, the increases in long hours of work, particularly among the more highly qualified, run counter to the development of work–life balance policies in the workplace. It is somewhat ironic that managers, who themselves worked long hours, sometimes expressed the view that more flexible arrangements to help work–life balance were the best approach for other workers (Yeandle et al., 2002). It is an area of work organisation that is being challenged, but without obvious effect.

Challenges have been made to the assumptions that underpin workplace cultures where long hours are expected (Bailyn, 1993). These assumptions have all been shown to be questionable (with evidence to the contrary): that long hours equals commitment, that productivity (per hour) is higher when hours are longer, and that productivity is higher for work which is visible. However, the practices continue despite the challenges, partly through business pressures, and employee and employer acceptance of these assumptions, but also because accurate measures of productivity are often unavailable and difficult to construct. Employees can, of course, work long hours for very different reasons, not all of which are attributable to the organisation of work or its culture (Crompton et al., forthcoming 2003).

Inequalities in the workplace

Is the current provision of flexible working arrangements associated with inequalities between employees and resentment? This is an important question. When these arrangements were discussed under the heading 'family-friendly policies', there were many fears, although little evidence, that single workers or those without children would resent special treatment being given to families. The change in terminology from family-friendly to work–life balance or work–life integration was part of an attempt to argue that employer provisions should be available to all employees, and not just to those with families – partly in order to minimise the risk of resentment.

Studies in this programme illustrate that employer fears persist despite the terminology. Dex and Scheibl (2002) recorded that some small employers who did not have any flexible arrangements, feared that introducing such arrangements would generate resentment about inequalities between employees. Surveys have also recorded these fears for a nationally representative sample of employers; for example, 43 per cent of employers in the DfEE Baseline Work–Life Balance Survey thought that work–life balance practices were unfair to some staff (Hogarth et al., 2001). The extent to which these fears were based on bad experiences, bad practices or misconceptions was not made clear.

The research projects in this programme that carried out in-depth investigations of the operation of flexible working in organisations, found little evidence of disruption or resentment about having flexible arrangements. There were a number of reasons for this. Many of the policies did not particularly favour parents, but were open to any employee (Yeandle et al., 2002; Bond et al., 2002; Phillips et al., 2002). In some cases, employees had the job of sorting out the flexibility they wanted themselves (Yeandle et al., 2002). This took away any sense of inequity or resentment. Overall, take-up tended to be low. This meant that there was little about which to feel resentful.

In the many private sector flexible organisations, the organisation of work was designed to make sure some employees did not suffer from others having flexibility. This happened less in the public sector. In other organisations, where decisions were made about an employee's request for flexibility according to a business case, individuals were only allowed flexibility when it was not going to be costly to the organisation (Dex and Scheibl, 2002). In other cases, employees did not take advantage of the flexibility offered, because they were worried about the potential effects of additional workload on their colleagues (Phillips et al., 2002). These constraints probably had a limiting effect on any resentment.

It was also the case that some employees' flexibility was accepted as part of their more highly qualified status. Other employees who did not have flexibility tended not to resent the fact that others had it since it often went alongside longer hours and more responsibilities (Dex and Scheibl, 2002; Yeandle et al., 2002). This kind of flexibility did not breach the norms of the workplace and so was accepted by all. This shows that some of the fears of employers about flexibility causing resentment are unfounded. The DfEE Baseline Work–Life Balance Survey also found that the proportion of employees, 26 per cent, who thought work–life balance practices were unfair (to people like them) was far less than employers' fears suggested.

There was a lot of concern voiced by employees and managers about the exercise of discretionary power by line-managers over who got to work flexibly (Yeandle et al., 2002; Bond et al., 2002). Managers with more experience were more likely to depart from the rulebook than recent incumbents (Bond et al., 2002). Having a manager with greater experience could work to the advantage of some employees, who had their needs met in a way that suited their individual circumstances. This was particularly helpful for employees who developed caring responsibilities for older adults (Phillips et al., 2002). However, employees with junior managers more wedded to the rules did not get the same treatment. Training can clearly help here. There is also a role for unions in making the implementation of flexible working more even (Bond et al., 2002).

Certainly, it is not the case that employees on the lower rungs of organisations are obviously or systematically treated worse than those higher up, or have less access to flexible working arrangements. Where formal policies were in place, they did not discriminate between workers on the basis of hierarchical or income level criteria. If, in practice, some employees were not able or eligible to take advantage of the provisions, it was more related to the employees feeling their job was unique (single accountant), indispensable (care workers, IT support), or not suited to being worked flexibly (e.g. IT support, lab technician). However, employees of different qualification levels do have access to different types of flexible working arrangements, but these also varied by type of occupation. For example, flexi-time was common among office staff, where it seems to work well without disruption. Highly qualified engineers were able to devise their own flexible schedules as part of their higher status, but then often worked longer hours. As mentioned above, there were differences in employee awareness about their organisation's provisions (Yeandle et al., 2002; Bond et al., 2002). This may lead to some inequities. Better employer–employee communication would help here, but there may be more radical solutions to this problem that are possible, as discussed below.

Where flexibility worked best and was integral to workplace culture and business objectives there were no problems of inequity, although there were differences in treatment (Dex and Scheibl, 2002). These forward-thinking employers had been aware of the potential problems and had devised arrangements, sometime over a period of time, that offered all employees some benefits. They also had clear rules for eligibility, based on reciprocity and being a good hard-working employee, rather than on personal circumstances or needing time off. Trust between employees and managers was also more evident and voiced where employees felt the arrangements worked well (Dex and Scheibl, 2002; Phillips et al., 2002). In larger organisations, arrangements often worked better where they were devised with employee involvement – bottom up rather than top down, building on partnership, good and open employer–employee communications (Yeandle et al., 2002).

The WERS survey suggested that employers who predominantly or wholly employ men were less likely to offer flexible working arrangements to their employees. This can be a source of inequity between employers. If one parent always takes time off for emergencies and it is most often the mother, employers of mothers (but not fathers) are also more likely to have to face any associated disruption costs, rather than employers who refuse to allow employees to have this flexibility. These conditions are not equitable or ideal.

Organisations and relocation

It is fairly common for larger organisations to relocate their higher-grade manager or professional workers from one site to another in order to increase their experience and offer an internal career structure. One study in this programme examined this type of relocation (Green and Canny, 2003) and its consequences for family life. It proved difficult to find any representative statistics about the extent of such practices among employers. This was partly because the concept of an employer-initiated relocation is not well-defined. It can be voluntary or compulsory from the employee's point of view, or some mixture of the two. There can be individual moves, or group moves when the employer decides to move the business, merge, or restructure. The relocation agencies that help employers to move their employees suggested relocation was undergoing changes, partly because increased numbers of women in the workforce made families less likely to want to move with the male partner's job. It was clear that employer-initiated relocations mainly affect professional and managerial employees.

The study of relocation also showed that few employers have subjected their practices to any thorough cost–benefit assessment. Relocation policies were not based on clear business rationales, more on tradition. Neither had these employers considered this aspect of organisation policy in relation to work–life balance issues. If work–life policies were on employers' agendas, it was likely to be under a heading different from relocation, or handled by a different department. Interestingly, the government's Work–Life Balance campaign also has not identified relocation as a work–life issue.

The increasing reluctance of some male employees to relocate was making employers consider the effects on families and 'trailing spouses', although there was a reluctance to face up to the issues. Some employees were expressing preferences to commute to the new site, rather than relocate. This was catching employer policies on the hop. The support that families could be offered to do this, rather than relocate, was not thought through.

As indicated in Chapters 3 and 4, the costs for employees' families of relocation could be substantial, although a few had found it to be a mainly positive experience, especially where the costs of removal had been met by the employer and the family had moved up the ladder in the housing market. Since there was relatively little variation between employers in the help offered to relocating employees, it was not possible to identify whether some employer policies work better for families than others. Certainly, having removal expenses paid was the minimum to which all employees felt entitled. Employers largely accepted responsibility for this cost. Where employees had experienced more than one relocation many had learned to cope with it, although research projects are likely to find only families who have survived for interviews. Where employers had paid relocation agents, employees had found them helpful.

Conclusions

Flexible working arrangements appear to be on the increase. Some employers have recognised the need to respond to changing family circumstances. Others have moved reluctantly down this path in response to their employees. The competition for talent has been a strong motivator for organisations to offer flexible arrangements in some sectors. In other sectors, where labour market pressures may be lower and there is no regular employer–employee communication, nor any union or employee representation, the desire of employees for greater flexibility has gone unheard. Employers were interviewed in this programme who claimed their employees did not want more flexible working arrangements. However, their employees told researchers that they did want them.

The research in this programme has added valuable new evidence to the issue of whether it pays employers to offer flexibility to their employees. Overall, the message is a positive one for flexible working arrangements. These tend not to reduce business performance and, under the right conditions, can indeed enhance performance and employees' views of their employer. Will this make any difference to employers? Those employers who are already reaping the benefits of flexible working arrangements can be reassured. Those who have allowed individuals to work flexibly, but have not offered it to all employees, can be encouraged to be bolder in their extension of new working arrangements to other or all employees. Those who are resistant to flexible working may need more of a push to try new ways of working.

The adoption, from April 2003, of the Work and Parents Taskforce recommendations may help. This new light-touch legislation gives parents of children under six a right to request flexible working and the employer a duty to give their request serious consideration. This new approach is in tune with the recommendations that came out of projects in this programme. It has the potential to get resistant employers to see for themselves that allowing individual employees to have more flexible working arrangements of their choice will not damage their business – and may even benefit it. It was the view of one of the projects in this programme that such an approach would work best and build more of a partnership between employers and employees if employee requests included a presentation of a business case. This proviso would facilitate the extension of such a scheme to any employee, rather than restricting it solely to parents of young children.

Some might argue that we should be able to advocate flexibility without the rationale of a business case. Even if the outcome were that there were no benefits, but also no large costs, there would still be a case for extending flexibility to employees, given that they like it. But even if there were costs, there may still be a social case for extending flexibility to employees when families could benefit: as was the case made for sickness pay, or holidays, and health and safety at work regulations. There is the long-term sustainability of families and the workforce to consider. Nonetheless, the business case evidence helps us to know if there are business costs to flexibility – important in the debate about apportioning any costs of flexibility between employers, employees and the general tax purse. On the whole, employer costs appear to be minimal and potential benefits possible from adopting employment policies and practices that pay attention to employees' work–life interests, as well as the 'bottom line'.

The studies in this programme have uncovered and reaffirmed some earlier findings: that some workplaces do not implement or communicate their policies, or create supportive cultures for their take-up. This shows that it is not just a matter of time passing that will help the implementation process and resolve some of the implementation problems. More action is needed. At the same time, the projects have themselves brought new findings to light.

It is possible to learn from the more customised approach of smaller businesses a way that may avoid some of the old chestnuts relating to implementation. Smaller businesses have shown that it is possible to move from informal discretion as the basis for employee access to flexible working, to explicit reciprocity "You help the business and the business will help you". This is a way of directing line managers away from their own values and towards a consideration of the business needs. Having fewer policies, but a single policy or stated ethos of approachability under which individuals needs can be addressed, gets away from individuals misusing policies.

Informal and discretionary practices were evident in all sizes and shapes of workplaces. They are certainly not restricted to small businesses, as has sometimes been implied. Is this something to regret and take steps to stamp out? One research team investigating union involvement concluded that it would be better to have clearer formal policies, less discretion and more systematised access to flexible working arrangements. Another team researching smaller businesses argued that informal arrangements had many benefits for customising the arrangements to suit the employee. In some ways, approaches need to be devised that retain the benefits of discretion, which clearly worked to employees' benefit where practiced by experienced and confident line managers. There needs to be more openness about practices and discretion. Some suggestions that might help and which are being tried in other organisations are listed below. Unions are well-placed to help develop such arrangements and keep an eye on potential inequities, as argued in Chapter 4, although they are represented now in a much smaller proportion of workplaces.

The increases in long hours of work, running counter to the development of work–life balance policies in the workplace, is an area of concern – not least because of its persistence and increase, despite rational challenge. Although it is most common at managerial levels, the effects are inevitably broader. Where such cultures dissuade lower-level employees from considering promotion to managerial posts, they are not necessarily rational personnel strategies. A long hours culture can be argued to be a mechanism of social and workplace control for higher-grade workers, who would not be prepared to work under stricter command and control management discipline. It can also give the illusion of having flexibility, but workers can feel that 'good employees' ought not to take advantage of it. On the other hand, even this limited flexibility in these sorts of environments does allow many fathers to take a more active role in their children's school events than might otherwise occur (e.g. sports days), so it is worth having.

The challenges that long hours of work generate are likely to continue. One can hope that further demonstration of the business case for reduced hours will help to chip away at the beliefs that sustain long hours of work. There is also some hope in the next generation's stated preferences, as recorded in surveys. In the 1990s, both young men and young women were indicating that they wanted their (adult) life to be involved not only in paid work but also in family and personal life (Brannen et al., 2001). We might look to the future talent wars between organisations, therefore, as one influence that might help to chip away at the long hours culture.

This programme of research has had its focus on family life. Employees are viewed, therefore, as workers and family members. However, much of the research based in workplaces has examined flexible working arrangements as they are available to all employees. This is partly because organisations' policy statements and criteria were usually specified as applying to all, with the exceptions of parental, maternity or paternity leaves. However, it has also been a plank of policy arguments to move to making the case for work–life balance for all, rather than advocating family-friendly policies, with their narrower focus on families. The evidence suggests that flexibility often makes business sense. The evidence itself was not tied to particular groups of beneficiaries. However, when one sees who does use the flexibility and who benefits, mothers constitute a disproportionate number.

This suggests that we need not feel shy of arguing the case for family-friendly policies. They are not disadvantaging businesses that offer them, nor are they producing large-scale resentment or inequities. However, if other groups can benefit from the same flexibility, even if those who want it are far fewer, then the same business case will apply and be a reason for extending flexible working to all who choose them. Extending the use of flexible working to fathers would strengthen the business case. If there are any disruptive effects from flexible working arrangements at workplaces where mothers predominate in the workforce, these would be shared across employers more equally if fathers, as well as mothers, took turns in addressing the issues of family life that are part of employees' responsibilities.

Access to flexible working arrangements has the potential to attract workers. This can be a bonus where there are staff shortages. However, where work is organised along lean production lines, to run with minimum staffing levels, flexibility can cause problems. Sickness and holidays can also cause problems in such contexts, which suggests that it is the organisation of work that needs to be reviewed, rather than flexible working being ruled out.

Policy implications

Policy implications from this programme that are more specifically concerned with employers are described below. They are largely suggestions to aid the spread of flexible working arrangements in a best practice way. More general policy issues are discussed in Chapter 5.

- Employers need to go beyond window-dressing and off-the-peg policy solutions.
- Customised solutions work best for employees. So, encourage an approach to the adoption of flexible working that is based on employees' requests. This ensures successful solutions that meet employees' particular circumstances.
- Involve employees in devising flexible solutions. This holds out an opportunity for greater employee partnership, initiative and autonomy, all of which can benefit the organisation of work and, ultimately, the business.
- Rather than bolting-on flexible working policies, employers will experience far greater benefits if they are prepared to take the chance to review their organisation of work. A consideration of how the current organisation of work contributes to employees' work–life problems also holds out the potential to uncover and tackle ineffective and low productivity working practices.

- Extend the Work and Parents' Taskforce approach, with its duty on employers to give serious consideration to employees' request for flexibility, to cover all employees, not just parents with a child under six. This sort of customised approach is needed especially for carers of older adults.
- Employers and government policy discussions need to bring employee relocation policies under the work–life umbrella. Employers should carry out more rigorous cost–benefit analyses of employee relocation, and convince themselves it is worthwhile. Ways of alleviating some of the ill effects of relocation also need to be investigated.
- It is important to allow flexibility to men and women in order to avoid the promotion of discrimination in favour of one group and to spread any costs more evenly between employers. If flexibility is linked to a business case, there is no justification for allowing some but not other social groups to benefit from it: this would also reduce the risk of inequalities growing wider.
- Encourage union involvement as a partnership in devising new and more flexible ways to work as outlined above.
- Encourage the spread of multi-skilling, teamwork, rotating sabbaticals in other teams, and systems of explicit reciprocity between employers and employees as the best foundation for flexible working and a route towards greater partnership in the workplace.
- Encourage better communication between employers, managers and employees, and transparent policies that have clear benefits and are less subject to employee resentment.
- Address the communication issues, so that employees and line-managers are aware of organisation policies. This may mean avoiding over-long lists of policies and confusing names. One approach would be to encourage the use of simple but highly publicised and over-arching policy frameworks, such as the Freedom to Work initiative developed by BT.
- Employers should consider carefully the fact that lean staffing may cost your business the goodwill of employees and, possibly, customer satisfaction.

3 The effects of paid work on family life

The relationship between paid work and family life has two mutual directions of influence: from paid work to family life and vice versa. We hear much in policy discussions about the effects or costs of family life, or its breakdown, on work through increased absence. We hear less about the effects of work on family life, although recent studies have noted the effects on individuals of insecurity and the intensification of work (Burchell et al., 1999).

Different disciplines have often given emphasis to one or other of these directions. For example, psychologists have examined the effects of work on family life. Economists' models have quantified the limiting effects on mother's paid work of having small children. Higher family income from sources other than the mothers' earnings has also tended to reduce mothers' labour-force participation, although this declined over time. Mother's own wage rates are the other major influence on their participation, with higher earners more likely to be at work.

Paying for substitute child care can be a cost that, in effect, reduces the woman's wage rate, it has therefore been assumed, although with little supporting empirical evidence, that child-care costs also limit women's labour-force participation. While giving a good overall picture of some general relationships, these earlier studies have told us relatively little about the decision-making processes that go on in households. This has been a large gap, reflecting in part the lack of detailed qualitative empirical research, and the failure to consider the role of fathers, as well as mothers. This programme has provided the opportunity for conceptual development in what it means to be a good mother or a good father, and in the different ways parents use the concept of family time. It has also investigated fathers' roles more extensively through interviews with fathers.

There are many areas where paid work can have an effect on family life. Earlier reviews of the research on these effects have pointed to associations that could spill over from the sphere of work to the home, or compensation effects whereby satisfaction is sought in one to offset dissatisfaction in the other (Edwards and Rothbard, 2000). Alternatively, some individuals separate work and family in order to prevent each sphere from influencing the other. Resource drain can occur if work leaves less energy to tackle home issues, and family–work conflict can also occur. New examples of many of these relationships have emerged from this programme's research.

One problem with examining the effects of paid work on family life is that paid work covers such a wide range of conditions and experiences: for example, different occupations, types of contract, industry settings and hours of work. Individuals bring their own work history and personality to the workplace, and may have worked in the same workplace for varying amounts of time. Unpacking some of the elements of paid work was one of the aims of the research, it turned out to be very important. These (and probably many other) dimensions of paid work all make a difference to individuals' experiences of the effects of paid work on family life.

Against this background, this programme has investigated a number of topics on the effects of paid work on family life. New findings have resulted on the following areas:

- the benefits and disadvantages of mothers working;
- what parents mean by being a good mother or father, and 'family time';
- fathers' views about the effects of mothers' and their own work on family life;
- the effects of the experiences and quality of paid work on family life;
- the effects of the quantity of paid work on family life;
- the effects of the scheduling of paid work on family life;
- the effects of coordinating child-care arrangements;
- outcomes for children from parents' work;
- the experiences of lone parents working and caring.

The benefits of working

Earlier research noted the benefits of money, independence, social contacts and personal identity to women (Martin and Roberts, 1984; Harkness et al., 1995). The majority of women interviewed in projects in this programme saw women's addition to household income as necessary, even though they were at significantly different levels of income. Some new benefits were cited over the course of these research projects (Reynolds et al., 2003; La Valle et al., 2002; Backett-Milburn et al., 2001; Mauthner et al., 2001). These are new findings to add to the literature. Benefits mentioned included:

- benefits to mental health;
- gives an important role model and message to children about the importance of work (cited mainly by lone parents);
- the opportunity to give to the community, make a difference, improve life for others;
- gives an opportunity to face a challenge, as opposed to 'wasting time' staying at home.

The beneficial effects to the family and partner cited by mothers included:

- both the mother and her children appreciated their time together more because it was limited;
- the mother could develop useful skills that could be carried over for use at home; for example, negotiating, time-management, information relevant to caring for older adults, computer budgeting and assertiveness;
- paid work allowed the children to have material goods, treats and holidays they would not get otherwise;
- paid work enabled the mother to share the financial needs of the family, although mothers did not identify themselves as breadwinners;

- working outside the home could enhance marriage relationships by generating topics of conversation, and even by developing skills the mother could teach her spouse.

Fathers' accounts of the spillover effects from the mother's work, from the studies that interviewed fathers, encompassed all the same points (La Valle et al., 2002; Reynolds et al., 2003; Mauthner et al., 2001).

In contrast to the benefits, mothers cited some of the negative spillover effects from their work. Again, male partners repeated most of these points about their partners in their separate interviews. However, male partners who were interviewed put greater stress on the negative elements. Negative spillovers noted included:

- irritability and bad moods with the family, especially after a bad day;
- impatience with children and their slow pace after the fast pace of work;
- lower quality of relationships at home because of stress at work;
- time with spouse being curtailed;
- having insufficient energy to respond to children's requests;
- children not liking parents working at the weekend or when they are ill;
- time with children being squeezed due to long hours of work (which could be part-time);
- work encroaching into the home, in some cases where the mother worked at home.

Being a good mother

Mothers' and fathers' reactions to the effects of the mothers' work on their family life were informed by what it meant to be a good mother (Reynolds et al., 2003; Skinner, 2003; La Valle et al., 2002; Backett-Milburn et al., 2001; Mauthner et al., 2001). A good mother can be summarised as one who 'is there' for the children, and who gives priority to children's over her own needs and, if the choice has to be made, over workplace demands. Although not all of the interviewees cited all of the qualities, the list included the following points.

- actively spending time rather than just passing time with children, and without being irritable;
- seeing the various stages of child development for oneself;
- forgoing housework in order to spend time with children;
- organising wider family activities and get-togethers;
- being available to talk and respond to children's requests;
- looking after children in crises or illness and addressing their problems;
- changing their child care if children were unhappy;
- providing stable care, not pillar-to-post care, with trusted adults;
- making children safe and secure;
- providing opportunities for young children to socialise with each other;
- making sacrifices for them if necessary, including being prepared to move house to areas of relative safety;
- attending school functions and events where the children participate;
- eating together as a symbol of being a family;

- making sure the children can have the material standard of living the mother aspires to, especially if the mother felt she had a relatively deprived childhood herself.

The responsibilities were recognised as varying over the life stages of children. The time of day 'being there' was necessary also varied. For primary school children, it was when they got home from school, or around tea-time. For older children and teenagers, it was later in the evening.

Work affected family life negatively, therefore, if it prevented mothers from being a good mother. On the whole, fathers did not expect, nor were they expected to be substitute 'good mothers', except in minor ways when regular arrangements fell down or crises occurred. This is quite a demanding list. It is not difficult to see why mothers feel burdened going out to work if they also accept the above, even in part, as norms of their role.

Fathers' views about family and their role

There has been far less research on fathers than mothers. As we saw above, fathers identified the same spillover effects from mothers' working as mothers themselves had done. They also had much the same view about what was a good mother, although there were differences between parents at the working hours boundary in how effective mothers were in fulfilling these ideals. Being a good father was described as follows.

- meeting the financial needs of his family;
- meeting their emotional and security needs, although to a lesser extent;
- spending time with the family.

Earlier and more recent small-scale and local studies identified the primary importance given by fathers to their role as a breadwinner, meeting the family's financial needs, (Burghes et al., 1997; Warin et al., 1999; Hatter et al., 2002), and this was found to be linked to their being higher earners in the majority of families (Burghes et al., 1997). It is perhaps not surprising, therefore, that fathers' views of themselves as breadwinners was confirmed from other small-scale studies in this programme, which found this view across socio-economic groups, in north and south England, and in both rural and urban communities in Scotland and England. It also applies across different ethnic minority groups of family business owners (Basu and Altinay, forthcoming 2003).

These findings support the view that fathers' breadwinner role is deeply embedded in their thinking, and is important to their integration within families. However, as mothers have been increasing their share of household income, fathers interviewed in this programme said they were pleased with the additions to household income and spending this brought.

Fathers' breadwinner role was also linked with offering emotional stability and security to partners and children in one of the studies (Reynolds et al., 2003). This emotion work, as it has been called, has been thought to be the preserve of women in other studies (Dunscombe and Marsden, 1993; Hochschild, 1990). However, some fathers in this programme saw their own role as impinging on family emotions, but partly as the provider of a stable family structure or framework, within which day-to-day emotional ups and downs could be played out. Hatter et al.'s recent study of fathers also found that fathers see themselves as having a wider set of roles (Hatter et al., 2002).

As well as challenging early studies about the gender of emotion work, the studies support earlier findings (Warin et al., 1999) about the gendered domestic division of work. The fact that mothers spend more time than fathers looking after children was evident in these, as in many other studies. Mothers evidently broadly accepted this division of labour (Reynolds et al., 2003; La Valle, 2002; Mauthner et al., 2001; Baines et al., forthcoming 2003). Some mothers, as in previous studies, also expressed the view that they did most of the domestic work. However, it seems that part of this claim is based on a discounting of men's contributions. Men regularly took responsibility for 'do-it-yourself' and gardening at home, but this work was not necessarily valued or counted into the calculations by women. Although it was not the focus of studies in this programme, many mothers appeared as managers of domestic and emotion work within families. It may be the case that the lack or low levels of management work by fathers, or their greater choice, may be partly responsible for mothers feeling they do more domestic work, as noted in other studies (see Hochschild, 1990).

Middle-class mothers wanted more companionship and conversation from their partners whereas working-class mothers wanted and appreciated more practical help (Reynolds et al., 2003). Fathers in the lower socio-economic groups were more likely than fathers in higher socio-economic groups to spend time caring for children while the mother was at work (La Valle et al., 2002). This applied to a large proportion of fathers where mothers worked atypical hours, although not where mothers were self-employed (Bell and La Valle, 2003; Baines et al., forthcoming 2003).

Fathers also saw the need for parents, including themselves, to spend time with their children, a point also noted in a study by Hatter et al. (2002). Some fathers, faced with the conflict between the breadwinner role and time with the family, had chosen the former, although not necessarily without feelings of regret, guilt or sacrifice at neglecting time with children (Reynolds et al., 2003). In some cases, spending time with children was seen as the mother's role, and it was less of a problem if the father was not present. However, some fathers had made sacrifices in their own careers in order to spend more time with their children at a certain point in their lives. They were found in the urban studies around London (Reynolds et al., 2003) and in the ethnographic studies of three rural areas (Mauthner et al., 2001), as well as another study outside of this programme (Hatter et al., 2002). While these studies have identified and mapped all of these different responses by fathers, a large-scale study is needed to disentangle the quantities of each, and the determinants of the varying responses by fathers.

Fathers felt constrained by workplace norms and culture (La Valle et al., 2002; Reynolds et al., 2003). More than a few fathers across the various studies expressed the view that men were not expected to take time off work for family, or express a wish to have flexibility in working. Some jealousy was expressed that women got a better deal in the workplace, because it was expected that they would arrange work to suit family life.

Fathers were more likely than mothers to take for granted that they could deserve and take time for themselves to spend on hobbies or interests. However, they also felt that children had constrained this time, but they did not give the impression, as mothers did, that the time was scarce and precious. Fathers did accept that mothers were entitled to the same time for themselves. But, clearly, mothers were less likely to take time for self and, in many cases, unlikely to express the need to do this.

Finally, and fundamental to fathers' views about their own roles was the claim that having a family and children had changed them. The impression given is that they changed from the laddish culture of the single, to being a responsible adult, and that this changed their attitude towards work and a career, a change also noted in Hatter et al.'s (2002) study of fathers.

> "Once you have a family, you get a sense of responsibility. When [my partner] told me she was expecting I thought 'crikey, I'd better get serious about the career'."
>
> Father, skilled job: Reynolds et al., 2003

This fits with the extensive empirical findings that married men and men with children do better in employment than single men (Akerlof, 1998). The debates are likely to continue of whether this is because men with more motivation and higher economic prospects are more likely to be selected into marriage and having children, instead of because men change their behaviour following marriage. However, the views expressed by some of the fathers interviewed in studies in this programme, although not based on longitudinal data, distinctly suggest that they saw themselves as having changed, rather than having been selected into family life. Thus, the earlier evidence from some sociologists (e.g. Furedi, 2001; Dench, 1996) and criminologists (Farrington et al., 2000) about the socialising and civilising effects of women and families on men also gains support from this research programme.

The quality of work experiences matter

The effects of work on family life have tended to be studied one dimension at a time: for example, by the number of hours worked, or by the occupational classification of the job. One study in this programme aimed to unpack the work experience and examine how variations in this experience affected family life (Reynolds et al., 2003), providing a new British analysis of this under-researched area. The study, comparing working mothers and their partners, in the very different organisational settings of public and private sector workplaces found that organisational cultures, occupational ethos and job dynamics all had the potential to influence family life and relationships. The sorts of jobs mothers did and, in particular, the extent to which they had autonomy or control in their jobs, also influenced the impact of work on family life. So facing pressures at work, having a bad day and facing emotionally demanding caring situations, for example in the health service, meant that the effects of work could be carried over into the home relationships.

"When you're tired, you've had a tough day at work and you're absolutely shattered and [my son] is saying 'mummy, come and play with me' and you haven't got the energy to get up and play with him, then you do start to think is it all worth it?"

Mother, senior manager, higher status, accountancy firm: Reynolds et al., 2003

Similarly, feeling powerless to change things at work, or frustrated with the way work was organised also led to problems being carried over into the home for some mothers and fathers.

Another significant finding was that mothers' approaches to the spheres of home and work affected the extent to which work was allowed to affect family life. Those called *connectors*, felt there were connections between home and work. They allowed work to spill over into family life. Those called *separators* thought they should be separate, not overlapping spheres. They took steps to try and prevent any carry-over from work to home. Many mothers who worked in the health service accepted an ethic of caring in the workplace that coloured their view of work, and then was carried over into home life where caring was also expected. However, in some families, fathers expressed preferences that had to be taken into account.

Some fathers did not want their partners to bring home even stories and conversations about work. Part of this prohibition may have been related to the fact that many mothers were working in caring jobs, which raised emotions that had to be managed. The extent to which mothers (and fathers) are connectors or separators needs to be established in larger-scale surveys. However, the findings suggest that the quality of work, as well as individuals' ways of relating the spheres of work and home matter in the extent to which work affects family life. This finding reinforces the conclusions of Chapter 2, that one important key in the work–life balance, which needs to be reviewed and prioritised, is the organisation of work.

The quantity of work matters

As well as the new findings about the quality of work mattering to the carry-over of work into home life, studies found that the quantity of work is also viewed by parents as affecting family life, and both mothers and fathers' relationships with children and with each other (Reynolds et al., 2003; La Valle, et al., 2002; Mauthner et al., 2001; Backett-Milburn et al., 2001). Fathers are known to work longer hours than mothers. The findings from representative surveys of parents in this programme found that 30 per cent of fathers and six per cent of mothers worked more than 48 hours per week (La Valle et al., 2002); the percentages were higher for self-employed parents (La Valle et al., 2002; Bell and La Valle, 2003). In some cases, mothers, but more often fathers hoped to compensate for their absence from home during the week by spending more time at the weekend. The concept of providing compensating quality time as a substitute for quantity time was one that was often described, although this term was not necessarily used by parents.

"By the time I get home I'm really tired from the journey but I always read bed-time stories to the children every night. It's our quiet time together and I can use this chance to find out what has happened in their day."

Mother, secretary, lower status, accountancy firm: Reynolds et al., 2003

"I make more effort with them. I have less time with them but I value that time with them. When you're at home with them all the time you take your time with them for granted, I have a much better relationship with them by going to work."

Mother, manager, intermediate status, accountancy firm: Reynolds et al., 2003

Where parents worked over 48 hours per week, 42 per cent of mothers and almost two-thirds of fathers thought that reading and playing with children was limited by work. Substantial proportions of parents also thought that other activities with children and family visits were also limited by working such hours (La Valle et al., 2002).

Long hours of work, which inevitably resulted in working at atypical times of day, were identified as a key pressure point for families that particularly affected fathers' relationships with children. The group of fathers most likely to work long hours – those in professional, managerial and some manual jobs – were the least likely to be involved in the care of their children or their children's activities. Some mothers and fathers were already expressing regrets about the length of their working hours and its effect on family life, given the relatively short time children are young (La Valle et al., 2000; Reynolds et al., 2003).

"I would love to spend my time with [my son] and I'm envious that [my partner] works part time so she has that extra time with him. I only get the weekends with him because by the time I get home from work he's in bed and I see him briefly for breakfast...But we depend on my salary to pay the mortgage and it's not an option for me."

Father: Reynolds et al., 2003

In the study of a nationally representative sample of parents, there was substantial preference among mothers for shorter hours for both themselves and their partner.

- Over three-quarters of mothers who worked over 40 hours per week would prefer to work shorter hours.
- Eighty per cent of mothers whose partner worked 49–59 hours per week wanted them to work shorter hours, and 85 per cent wanted shorter hours for their partner where the partner worked over 60 hours per week.

The main reason given for this preference was in order to have more family time (La Valle et al., 2002). A survey of a nationally representative sample of employed mothers in 2001 found two-thirds saying that they wanted to work fewer hours (Woodland et al., 2002). In the same survey, just under half (44 per cent) of employed mothers, a surprisingly high percentage, said that they would prefer to give up work to stay at home with their children, were they able to afford it. Other studies have also noted a decline in mothers' interest in paid jobs after a baby is born, compared with before (Houston and Marks, 2000). Many found they wanted to spend time with the child. This study found that when a baby was 12 months old, mothers who were both full and part-time employees displayed higher levels of distress than those who were not employed. It is indicators like these that suggest, although families are appearing to cope with the pressures of having two employees, that the strain on mothers of this life-style is high.

Fathers' reasons for working long hours varied (La Valle et al., 2002; Reynolds et al., 2003). The professionals and managers were driven more by a sense of career ambition and a desire to have a sense of personal achievement. These could be fuelled by loyalty to an employer or, in the case of the self-employed, wanting to build up a successful business. Among employees, this was sometimes because of paid overtime and the job demanded this, but sometimes there was no extra pay for the long hours worked. In these cases, men thought they would be rewarded for their commitment through promotion or better career prospects.

Cases of men who had opted out of such jobs were found in the three rural areas studied, the 'downshifters' (Mauthner et al., 2001). Fathers who had given up the prospect of promotion in order to put their family first were also found in urban-based studies (Reynolds et al., 2003). However, for the majority of fathers who worked long hours this was associated with giving higher priority to their family's material standard of living, and was part of their breadwinner role. Almost identical views were expressed by both professional and skilled manual fathers, as these two quotations illustrate.

> *"You want them to have a good life...I work to provide them with a nice home, nice clothes and a decent education."*
>
> Father, professional: La Valle et al., 2002

> *"All the long hours I work is for them, so they can have nice things and they don't go without"*
>
> Father, skilled: La Valle et al., 2002

Long hours could also be associated with other features of workplaces, levels of pay and attitudes. In some cases, fathers were working long hours in jobs in which they were unhappy, in order to give their family a better standard of living. They felt they were making personal sacrifices for the benefit of the family.

Patterns of working time matter

Atypical work, outside the 9 to 5, Monday to Friday time, has been growing alongside the pressure to have a 24/7 society, as noted in Chapter 1. The nationally representative study of parents in this programme, which focused on the effects of such work, found a large number of different patterns occurring for a variety of reasons (La Valle et al., 2002). The sense of whether there was a choice about the atypical work made a big difference to the effects parents perceived this type of work to have on their family life. When parents had chosen these types of working arrangements and the hours of atypical work were relatively short, atypical work tended to be perceived as beneficial, allowing more time with children.

A large group of self-employed mothers had specifically chosen this form of employment as a way of combining work and family life (Bell and La Valle, 2003). Where parents felt they had little choice over their working arrangements and worked substantial atypical hours, the effects on family life were seen as primarily negative. One study noted more awareness among fathers than mothers who were working long hours of the potential damage to children caused by their hours of work (Reynolds et al., 2003).

Parents who frequently worked atypical hours, whether one or both, also were more likely to think that family activities and overlapping family time were limited by paid work.

- Thirty-two per cent of mothers who frequently worked atypical hours, and 46 per cent of fathers, said that every week their work limited the time they could spend reading with, playing with or helping children with their homework, compared with 12 per cent of mothers and 18 per cent of fathers with more standard working hours (La Valle et al., 2002).

Most of these mothers and fathers were dissatisfied with this state of affairs. The government expects parents to be more involved in supervising children's homework, and now insists on homework being given in primary schools. The trends towards greater amounts of atypical work run counter, therefore, to the demands on parents to be more involved with children's education.

Working atypical hours also impinged on family outings and the frequency of being able to share a family meal (La Valle et al., 2002). Again, most of those who felt their family life was affected in these ways by atypical work were dissatisfied with this situation. Families clearly tried to prioritise children's needs and time was spent with children in order to protect them from any ill effects as a result of working at atypical times. Parents who adopted this pattern as a way of coping with child care – sometimes setting up shift-parenting schedules – were prepared to put their partner's and their own needs clearly second to their children's needs (La Valle et al., 2002; Reynolds et al., 2003; Skinner, 2003; Mauthner et al., 2001). While this could be a benefit to children, studies found (La Valle et al., 2002; Reynolds et al., 2003) the following:

- fathers expressed sadness and dissatisfaction with the time they spent as a couple;
- parents who both frequently worked atypical hours expressed the greatest dissatisfaction about time couples had together. This group were most at risk of pressures on their marriage or partnership from work.

Lone parents experienced many difficulties through working atypical hours. The combination of substantial atypical work, lack of choice or control over working arrangements and limited access to child care was particularly problematic for this group of parents (La Valle et al., 2002; Backett-Milburn et al., 2001).

Weekend work

The surveys and even qualitative interviews (La Valle et al., 2002) suggested that the vast majority of mothers were dissatisfied with, in order of importance:

- working long hours;

- working on Sundays;
- working on Saturdays.

"They don't mind about me going to work unless it's the weekend when they'd like to go somewhere and I say 'Oh, I've got to go to work today'. Then they really moan."

Mother, clerk, lower status, hospital: Reynolds et al., 2003

Strong preferences for changes of hours were expressed by mothers working all of these patterns and times. Mothers also expressed strong preferences for fathers to change their working patterns and hours when they were working long hours, or on Sundays or Saturdays (La Valle et al., 2002). Weekend work is particularly a problem once children have reached school age. Government considerations of working time regulations need to pay attention to these findings, as discussed more fully in Chapter 5.

Interestingly, the programme's study of child-care provision at such times found strong views expressed from providers of child care that children needed to be with their families at weekends (Statham and Mooney, 2003). This overlaps with the majority of parents' views (La Valle et al, 2002).

Child care

The patterns of hours of work have to interface with child-care arrangements. A detailed study of how parents coordinate and transport their children to care locations was undertaken in one of the programme's projects (Skinner, 2003). This study revealed the extraordinary complexity of some of the arrangements that parents set up in order for both parents to be able to work in two-earner or 1.5-earner families. One example was documented in full (see Box 2, page 66).

The complexity derives from several factors: different caring establishments have different opening and closing times, which do not always coincide with the start and finishing times of work, thus children have to be transported to and from, and sometimes between different forms of care. Younger children need 'wrap-around' care. Having children of different ages causes additional complexity because of the way education and child care are organised in Britain, they can rarely be cared for in the same establishment or at the same location. The geography of these types of provision is crucially important to their viability. Parents' preferences about the care they thought best added another element of complexity to this picture. Skinner's study (2003) of the details of child-care arrangements in 40 families revealed that *coordination* is an important and neglected element in considerations of child care.

Outcomes for children

What are the effects on children of mothers' and fathers' paid work? Earlier studies found that children's education and ability, their emotional development and, to a lesser extent, their use of illegal substances and other criminal activity are all affected by the nature of parental employment (Haveman and Wolfe, 1995). However, studies that have found an association, at a specific point in time, between certain forms of parental behaviour and some outcome measures for children are not satisfactory for policy purposes because they do not identify the causal sequence. It is not clear from such studies whether the work causes the outcome for children, or the child's outcome causes the parent's behaviour as a response to it.

Over time, more studies have used longitudinal data to try to find out which are the causal factors that explain the outcomes. This raises statistical challenges and a range of outcomes are being investigated. Parenting is a tricky process, and parents differ widely in their parenting styles and practices. Surveys cannot hope to ask questions about and record all of the differences between parents. Perhaps it does not matter. Perhaps there are only some fairly major elements to parenting, parents' behaviour and parents' circumstances that really affect the outcomes for children. The trouble is that we do not know which they are. The history of attempts to explain children's educational achievements illustrates some of the problems.

There has been a long-standing debate about the effect of parental employment on children's educational performance over a range of disciplines. A review of these studies found that the methods used to evaluate these effects are very varied (Haveman and Wolfe, 1995). Not surprisingly, the conclusions varied by type of data and type of approach. Some earlier British evidence, based on longitudinal data, found a positive relationship between the employment of mothers and children's educational achievement (Ermisch and Francesconi, 1997; Kiernan, 1996). However, these studies did not control for all the unmeasured elements that go into parenting.

The advent of longitudinal survey data about siblings brought up in the same household provided a rare and valuable opportunity for researchers in this programme to consider these issues further and be first in analysing the outcomes for children of parents' employment, after controlling for all the unobservable things that go into parenting. The study found some negative effects on children's education from mothers having worked, especially full-time, when the child was of pre-school age (Ermisch and Francesconi, 2001). Other studies have found overlapping findings, although they have not been able to use such sophisticated and robust techniques. Fathers' employment over the course of the children's lives was not found to vary sufficiently to have any explanatory significance on their education and other outcomes.

What this study fails to be able to examine is what happened to the children in their pre-school years, while their mother was working. This issue has been aired in other studies and reviews, but in a way that has failed to reach firm consistent conclusions. This is obviously a crucial area for policy to pursue, although one where data are not currently available in sufficient quantities to be able to cast light on it.

The experiences of lone parents

Lone parents have been a growing group in the population of families, but are less likely to be in paid employment, especially lone mothers. We also knew at the outset of the programme that they are more likely to have health problems, and have fewer educational qualifications than mothers in couples (Holtermann et al., 1999). The programme included one study that focused specifically on employed lone parents in the lower socio-economic groups with primary school-aged children, in order to find out how this relatively unusual and unresearched group experienced work and care (Backett-Milburn et al., 2001). It was possible that insight would be gained into why other lone parents do not take up paid work – over and above the well-known reasons relating to the benefit system disincentives, combined with low earning power and high child-care costs. In addition, other research projects in the programme included lone parents, even though they were not the particular focus of interest (La Valle et al., 2002; Mauthner et al., 2001; Skinner, 2003). There are potentially important findings about lone parents to note from all of these studies, although in some cases, the more tentative findings need to be replicated and tested out on larger samples.

The national survey (La Valle et al., 2002) showed employed lone mothers in comparison with employed partnered mothers:

- work at atypical times of day, frequently to the same extent as their partnered equivalents;
- if they work at atypical times of day they are less likely to do so for the reason of ease of child care;
- more likely to have no choice about their hours and time of day at work;
- more likely to use informal child care;
- more likely to eat an evening meal every day with their children;
- less likely to have an annual holiday of a week or more;
- more likely, if they worked atypical hours frequently, to say that it often interfered with family activities, such as reading, playing and recreation, although not with outdoor activities or family visits;
- more likely to be dissatisfied with the amount of time available to spend with children.

The group of employed lone parents showed enormous determination to work (Backett-Milburn et al., 2001). Many felt very strongly that they did not wish to be dependent on state benefit. They also wanted to be seen as reliable workers, having a good record on absence. It is possible that these attitudes, based on a strong sense of independence, are ones that mark these lone parents out from those who decide not to work. At the same time, this group of employed lone parents expressed motivation to give high priority to their child's needs.

It was clear that many of the group of employed lone parents were living on a tightrope of pressure and stress in their attempts to cope with a job and care for children (Backett-Milburn, 2001). There was an enormous rate of job changing over a 6-month period. This finding needs testing on a bigger sample, to see if lone parents are more likely to change jobs and have shorter job tenure.

Many lone parents expressed feelings of guilt about their working and caring lives. Clearly, they shared with all parents the problems of juggling work and care, especially in times of crises through children's illness, ad hoc changes in the school timetable, and school holidays. They had fewer resources of income and back-up from a partner on which to draw, but the same was also true of some of the partnered women in this socio-economic group whose partners were not expecting to help (Backett-Milburn et al., 2001).

On the other hand, like many women with children, lone parents had cultivated networks of other parents who they could ask for help, and sometimes offer help to in a form of reciprocal exchange (Backett-Milburn et al., 2001; Skinner, 2003; La Valle et al., 2002). These relationships were used to provide child care, but were experienced as fragile – although providing necessary flexibility. They felt unable to have other children round after school because the lone mother was at work and the child cared for by another adult (Backett-Milburn et al., 2001). However, it was the child and his or her friendships that were felt to suffer most from this situation. This problem was probably not exclusive to lone parents, although it may be less severe in the case of two-parent families who, between them, may be able to both work and provide for some social occasions for the child to meet other children at home.

Conclusions

Family life is central to fathers and mothers. Family life affects parents' identity, their levels of fulfilment and satisfaction, their motivation for work and their sense of responsibility. Fathers' and mothers' choices about work and working hours are often made with their children's needs in mind, although parents differ in the needs they prioritise. Couples' needs for each other tend to be of lower priority than children's needs. However, because of the different priority attached to the family's material well-being, some fathers think that time spent in relationship-building in families is more important than a higher standard of living, career progression at work and longer-term prospects. These fathers are prepared to stick at jobs without prospects, sometimes with lower pay, or to move area to achieve a better balance at the expense of their material standard of living. Fathers who work long hours tend to rely on mothers to provide what they see as the necessary time input into children.

Parents' views about the effects of work on family life heavily revolved around the financial benefits and their view of child care. Satisfactory child-care arrangements varied with the age of the child. Children made their voices heard on this issue, and parents had to listen to them (Backett-Milburn et al., 2001 Baines et al., forthcoming 2003). While there was this priority attached to the needs of children, there was still a recognition that a host of other factors were involved in both mediating and determining the effects of work on family time. From the perspective of the home, the factors that were important included children's commitments and activities, the journey-time to work, whether the woman had a supportive partner, and attitudes that generally varied by socio-economic group. Hobbies or interests were also important factors. Workplace factors, in particular, workplace cultures and practices, and the levels of autonomy and control workers felt they had in the workplace, were also important.

Certain types of jobs make parents' responsibilities more difficult to fulfil. Working at atypical times of day or working long hours can be a problem if work coincides with times when children are at home, or on holiday and not at school. Unsympathetic line managers made parents' lives more difficult. Mothers expressed a very strong desire to change weekend work, and long hours of their own and their partner. Where there is no flexibility at work, parents cannot show their interest in their children through school events or supporting their homework. School timetables that change can also be a problem for parents: for example, when training days and occasional school closures occur. Coordination of child-care arrangements through the day and the week, and its associated geography – especially where there was more than one child – led to some extraordinarily complicated journeys to and fro on the part of parents, and other paid and unpaid carers (Skinner, 2003). The extent of these problems needs to be examined through national surveys.

Working patterns have been moving in the direction of increased atypical work for both men and women. The study in this programme revealed that this pattern of working can have serious negative implications for family life. However, it could also be a choice, like self-employment is for some women, that enables them to combine work and family life in a way which more or less completely suits them. Technically, it is the case that atypical work does not have to have bad effects on family life. But examining the numbers, it is fairly clear that it is a privileged few for whom the solution to work and care is atypical work. By far the majority are facing little choice and more of the negative effects on family life.

Policy implications

Some policy implications follow from the findings of these projects, as discussed below and again in Chapter 5. Policy issues relating to child-care provision for parents working during atypical hours are also discussed in Chapter 4.

If the government is keen on parents working, as it seems to be, there are a number of difficulties that disrupt parents' work which, if addressed, could lead to a smoother ride for working parents.

- Serious policy attention needs to be paid to the coordination issues and their associated geography, which parents face in trying to arrange child care for children of different ages in different care and educational establishments.
- Ensure that schools, even though they are now independent, are not allowed to change their schedules at short notice.
- Organise child care on site at school for training days, at low cost. Although parents in principle can organise this between themselves, it is far more efficient for the school to organise this.
- Encourage the growth of a wide variety of holiday child-care services and clubs.

Parents' strong and widespread dissatisfaction with Sunday working has implications for policy and the regulation of Sunday trading. Although jobs in retail and associated jobs are not the total of Sunday work, there clearly has been an extension of Sunday work since Sunday shop-opening hours were extended in 1994 to six hours per day (Hill and

Dex, 1999). Extending the opening hours of shops further, a case that is being advanced by some large retailers, can only make this worse. Governments who say they are interested in helping families will not be fulfilling their objectives by facilitating or advocating the further increase of Sunday or other weekend work, whether this be by complete deregulation of Sunday trading, or through other public services being made available on Sunday, if it means more parents will work on Sunday.

In fact, on the basis of the current feelings of parents who carry out this weekend work, there needs to be serious consideration given to reducing the current levels of parents' needs to work on Sunday. Of course, the income needs of families must be considered in this discussion. Giving families the choice to avoid Sunday work, but no choice to increase their earnings at other times, may not be a choice at all.

Similar strong negative feelings about very long working hours are expressed by the majority of parents involved. The implementation of the Working Time Directive was meant to limit working hours. Nonetheless, studies in this programme found that many fathers still work over 48 hours per week and are unhappy with their long hours. Again, the extent to which this is driven by income needs, or by choice and career ambitions, needs to be considered in any further discussions about changes to the regulations.

4 Partnerships and supports

The Joseph Rowntree Foundation's Work and Family Life research programme set out to examine families and work and see how families are coping in the changed environment. There was specific interest in families' relationships to the wider community. But community partnerships with families are only one aspect of partnership and support for family life. On this topic of family relationships with paid work there are at least four areas for support. Workplaces can provide support for families, over and above paying wages for work carried out. Workplace-based institutions like trade unions can support families by protecting their employment conditions or negotiating more family-friendly working conditions and arrangements. There can be personal and household resources upon which families draw. There can be a local infrastructure that can support and facilitate families. These are all areas of partnership that can help support family life at the frontier with the workplace.

This chapter first considers the non-market or quasi-market partnership developments that may support family life, which came to light through these research projects. Market-based solutions to support working parents covered in this chapter are mainly concerned with child-care provision, although not all child care is provided in a market context, as discussed below. In considering these areas of partnership we begin to touch more directly on policy and the implications from this programme's findings. Further discussion of policy on some broad, general, but in places overlapping, issues also takes place in Chapter 5.

New findings and potential for partnerships were found in this programme's research projects under the following headings:

- partnerships relating to employers;
- the role of trade unions;
- child-care partnerships;
- other family–community partnerships;
- family business and ethnic minority communities.

Partnerships relating to employers

A number of general findings emerged from these examinations of partnerships.

- Employees and families draw heavily on their own resources. Family businesses are a particular example of where family, work and sometimes home are most integrated, although not necessarily free of problems.
- Very few employers have effective links with, or information about local sources of infrastructure, be that child-care providers, or services related to caring for older adults.

- Support for families exists, but links need to be made, possibly via the workplace, to facilitate greater support for working carers.

As indicated above, the market has increased the supply of child care, but information about these provisions is not necessarily widespread. This lack of information and local knowledge was obvious in the case of families who moved areas with their employer, either compulsorily, or voluntarily (Green and Canny, 2003). But the information gap was evident in other cases, encompassing help with caring for older adults, as well as children.

The need for better links

There is help in the community, through Social Services, for older adults in need. Hardly any of the working carers of older adults had accessed this help when they needed it most (Phillips et al., 2002), in some cases, through lack of information. Human resources specialists could keep information and leaflets of where to go for help to inform carers who are facing crises.

The Social Services department studied said it had many links with organisations relevant to working carers of older adults, but did not make use of these links in addressing the needs of working carers (Phillips et al., 2002). Even simple actions like putting people in touch with relevant organisations were rarely considered. Neither did managers in this organisation draw on the assistance of their own organisation's Elder Care Directorate. The barriers that were cited as preventing the potential for partnerships to be realised were: costs, issues of confidentiality, difficulties working with other agencies, and the lack of being prepared to take the initiative. Work needs to be carried out to address these issues, and to provide models of good and effective information transfer and communications between and within different types of institutions.

Some employers now subscribe to web-site based information about local child-care providers and school holiday provision. Employees have found such services helpful.

Initiatives

In the regions covered by this programme's research projects, examples of initatives and organisations were found that benefited both employers and employees. Organisations providing information about child care have been springing up, in some cases with government contracts to develop local web-based coverage of child-care provision throughout Britain (Dex and Scheibl, 2002).

One Sheffield-based organisation was described that is a partnership between the local authority and other agencies, and is supported by funding from the European Social Fund (Yeandle et al., 2002). This organisation is willing to help develop child-care businesses, support family-friendly employment and work–life balance initiatives, run business clubs, work with employers and has a web-site and resource packs.

A similar web-based organisation covering many of the same functions was found in Essex (Dex and Scheibl, 2002). There are also longer-standing national organisations with overlapping functions aiming to support working parents. Agencies offering information and help with child care to employers have been springing up all over Britain. For a modest subscription, employers can allow their employees access to the use of these services.

"A large employer came to us for advice about absence problems in the school holidays. We linked them with various out-of-school clubs and looked at partnering them for a holiday playscheme. We assist companies to become responsible for child-care growth opportunities include offering management training on family-friendly working."

Yeandle et al., 2002

The funding for some of these initiatives has been kick-started from public funds. This can sometimes lead to problems. Researchers heard, after their field-work period was over, that one of those initiatives was struggling, having had its funding removed by changes in the structures, budgets and relationships of local government agencies in the late 1990s, before it had reached the point of being a sustainable business. One could argue that it would have been better to give support from public funds for longer. However, some other companies offering services for family support have become successful without any injection of public funds. Such companies would see the injection of public funds into other businesses as destroying the level playing field for competition.

The same issues are arising in the provision of child care, especially for care at atypical times of day, for which public subsidies have been available for the first year of operation. Statham and Mooney's (2003) consideration of some innovative schemes found they faced problems of business viability at the end of their one year of subsidised funding. A recent evaluation study of the business support offered to start childcare businesses revealed that the support is often patchy or non-existent (Osgood, 2003). One lesson to be learnt is that more careful consideration is needed, at the outset, of business plans, marketing strategies and assessments of demand for childcare. The business support service needs to become more effective.

Learning and sharing networks
Studies found some partnership initiatives developed by employers. One study found an innovative small business owner who had adopted a wide range of flexible working arrangements, and had started up a learning and sharing network for employers in the area (Dex and Scheibl, 2002). The organisation in question was clearly committed to what the management literature calls being *a learning organisation*. This network held dinners and meetings. At least two other employers were known to have taken up and be implementing ideas they had heard at these meetings.

It is interesting to ponder on why this network was being successful when years of government-sponsored initiatives of this kind have produced little and been generally regarded as being a failure. It may be because this network was employer initiated. Certainly, studies have found small businesses are often antagonistic to government initiatives, feeling that they are modelled on large employers and not sensitive, therefore, to the needs of small business. Small business owners feel unable to own many of the initiatives that come out of central or local government for this reason. One conclusion is that successful and effective networks may need to be employer-led.

Employer–agency communication

Local agencies in the Eastern region were eager to help employers develop family-friendly and flexible employment policies (Dex and Scheibl, 2002). However, it was hard to reach them. Few employers turn up to meetings or other events where they are organised by local or regional government agencies. It was not possible to find any small local employers who were willing to take the offer of £1000 to spend on a care audit for their workforce in the late 1990s. Local or regional agencies need to develop ways of talking to local employers that do not take up much of their precious time.

More successful communication may also occur if local agencies work through one employer to reach another, not unlike the pyramid selling techniques some marketing agents now use for retailing. The possibility of more web-based and e-communication needs to be explored. However, employers told researchers that face-to-face communication is the best, certainly in the first instance. But clearly, a degree of confidence building and trust is also needed. Small employers need to be convinced that these agencies have something to offer and deliver. The regular changes in local government and its personnel were found to have negative effects on the development of relationships between local agencies and local employers.

The message to employers is that there are regional and local agencies eager to encourage, and even offer resources and assistance to help employers change and adopt more flexible working arrangements that are appropriate to their business needs.

Role of trade unions

According to survey evidence, trade unions have been playing a role in the development of flexible working arrangements in British organisations. This is the reverse of the USA, where flexible working has developed outside of the area of trade union organisation and recognition. Flexible working arrangements are more common in Britain, where trade unions are recognised in the workplace (Dex and Smith, 2002). However, the qualitative and in-depth interviews with employers in the financial services sector in Scotland down-played the union's role in the initiation and motivation to develop the policies (Bond et al., 2002). It was recognised, however, that unions had played a role in their implementation of flexible working policies and practices.

It is in this area of practice and implementation that unions have an obvious role to play. Two studies suggested that there is potential for unions to play a greater role in the implementation of policies (Bond et al., 2002; Houston and Waumsley, forthcoming 2003). There is a clear role for unions, therefore, in several areas.

- The communication and awareness gap that exists between employees and employers. Awareness of employers' policies is already better where there are recognised unions and among union members rather than other employees (Bond et al., 2002; Yeandle et al., 2002).

- Plugging the awareness gap of line managers about their employer's policies and issues of work–life balance. Part of the reason there is more awareness where unions are recognised is that unions make employers codify the policies (Bond et al., 2002).
- Pressing employers to provide more training for line managers.
- Pressing for clearer relationships and communication channels between human resources specialists, line managers and employees.
- Helping to implement policies with equity.
- Making sure employer's policies address the needs of employees. This is an area where unions have a comparative advantage, since they are already placed in this intermediary position with potential to talk to both sides. The TUC has been doing innovative work at this interface, facilitating the development of more grounded flexible working arrangements – grounded, that is, in employees' preferences, but also addressing business or service needs (TUC *Changing Times* website).
- Reducing the construction of policies that are either merely window-dressing, or off-the-peg policies that do not address employees' needs.

In order to fulfil these roles, unions will have to provide training to their own shop stewards and representatives (Houston and Waumsley, forthcoming 2003). Studies of union roles in this programme found that there was often enthusiasm and recognition of the issues at central HQ, but that further down the line there was less awareness and a view that the concerns at the centre were all talk rather than action (Houston and Waumsley, forthcoming 2003; Bond et al., 2002).

The implementation of the Work and Parents Taskforce recommendations from April 2003, giving the right to parents with a child under six years old to request flexible working arrangements, facilitates the sort of intermediary partnership role for unions that is being advocated above. Unions could have an important role in the processes of:

- increasing awareness of this new possibility;
- developing customised solutions to employee requests within the context of the business concerns;
- helping employees to present their requests and indicate how they could work in practice;
- helping to ensure they get serious and fair consideration;
- helping in the presentation of an appeal, where a refusal of flexibility is felt not to be just or reasonable.

Child-care partnerships

Sorting out satisfactory care for children is integral to the decision to go out to work and has to be solved alongside the decision to work. This is an area of partnership between parents themselves, between parents and relatives, friends and neighbours, or between parents and other child-care providers. The increase of mothers in paid work has led to an increased need for child care by non-parental carers.

The use of paid or formal types of child care has not grown at the same pace as mothers' increases in paid work, although it has increased. In the early 1980s, 30 per cent of employed mothers who made arrangements for pre-school children (48 per cent of full-timers and 22 per cent of part-timers) used paid care for some of the working week; 10 per cent of women who made arrangements for school children during term-time paid for care (16 per cent of full-timers and seven per cent of part-timers) (Martin and Roberts, 1984). At the start of the twenty-first century, of those mothers who made arrangements for pre-school children, approximately 50 per cent of them paid something for this care (Woodland et al., 2002).

Judicious choice of hours of work by mothers working part-time and fathers can sometimes cover the child care without engaging the market sector and even, in some cases, without recourse to informal arrangements. This pattern is known as *shift parenting* but it is used as a strategy by only a minority of dual earner families; 29 per cent of partnered mothers who worked atypical hours did so in order for their partner to be able to look after the children (La Valle et al., 2002). Fathers' general participation in caring for children is much greater than in the 1980s, as time budget studies have also noted, and more so where there were atypical working hours. As many as 30 per cent of fathers in two-parent households provided some child care in families where both parents worked atypical hours, compared with 10 per cent of fathers in families where neither parent worked atypical hours.

Child care is one of the pervasive themes in the research projects in this programme. Set against the background of a newly devised National Child Care Strategy, it is a sensitive area that evokes emotion, defensive responses and even guilt in some working mothers. All of these were displayed in the responses to questions about how mothers combine work and care (Backett-Milburn et al., 2001; Mooney et al., 2001; Reynolds et al., 2003; Crompton et al., forthcoming 2003). However, in asking specifically about the benefits to children, as well as potential disadvantages, many themes emerged. These were described in Chapter 3 as the experiences of work and care.

From qualitative interviews with many mothers in these studies, it became clear that the majority of those interviewed placed highest priority on their children being happy in their child-care settings (Backett-Milburn et al., 2001; Mooney et al., 2001; Reynolds et al., 2003; Mauthner et al., 2001). One important finding was how powerful children's voices can be if they are expressing unhappiness or dissatisfaction with day care, after school or holiday care, with work intruding into the home or taking up a lot of parental time (Backett-Milburn et al., 2001; Baines et al., forthcoming 2003). One study interviewed children to hear their voices directly (Baines et al., forthcoming 2003).

Children themselves are one of the stress factors for parents, alongside pressures at work, and the needs of managing the home. Another finding was that younger children, especially pre-school, are often easier to satisfy than older children, late primary school children and teenagers. Pre-school care can usually be obtained to cover the working day and holiday periods. But the school day imposes new inflexible timetables, causing coordination problems, and long and inflexible holiday periods (Skinner, 2003; Yeandle et al., 2002; Backett-Milburn et al., 2001; Mauthner et al., 2001).

However, the unhappiness of children, while it required parents to adapt and, in some case, change the child-care arrangements, rarely led to complete cessation of working. The group of lone parents with primary school children appeared to change their jobs very frequently in response to child-care issues (Backett-Milburn et al., 2001), but these were parents in lower socio-economic group occupations where turnover and change is more frequent (Burgess and Rees, 1996).

Child care and the self-employed

The study of self-employed parents in large-scale representative surveys and through qualitative interviews led to some interesting perspectives on working and caring. While the personal characteristics of the self-employed have been well documented, the relationship of self-employment to family life and care issues has received very little research attention. (Bell and La Valle, 2003). Child care figured very strongly in many self-employed mothers' reasons for being self-employed, especially where they were self-employed without any employees. The self-employed parents without employees are a population made up of two groups; the highly qualified minority (16 per cent) and the manual majority (57 per cent).

The picture emerging of the manual majority is one of mothers solving their need for income by becoming self-employed, working part-time, gaining flexibility and control over their work and managing with informal or parental child care (Bell and La Valle, 2003; Baines et al., forthcoming 2003). The self-employed with employees were found to be a more highly qualified group, and made use of a mixture of informal and formal paid child care that had more parallels with their employee counterparts, although with a higher proportion using formal child care, in keeping with their higher qualified status.

Affordability availability and quality of child care

The cost of child care was discussed by parents. Many needed to budget tightly to meet child-care costs. Parents expressed different attitudes towards the cost of child care, varying according to their socio-economic group or income. For the low paid there has to be a reasonable immediate return to the effort involved in working. Mental calculations are performed by mothers; child-care costs are subtracted from the net weekly wage and the decision made as to whether it is worth working. It has to make sense on a weekly basis.

> "Well, there the Easter holidays coming up and the Childcare Centre, I've not got worked out what I need him in. Like, if I was putting him in all day every day, I mean, it wouldnae be worth my while working."
>
> Lone parent, Backett-Milburn et al., 2001

For middle class or higher income mothers, child-care costs may be high now, but they are seen as short term and a necessary investment in the mothers' own future careers and income levels (Reynolds et al., 2003; Yeandle et al., 2002; Crompton et al., forthcoming 2003).

Childminders and parents referred to the niggling over-payment when childminders were not being used because of days off or holiday (Mooney et al., 2001). Lone parents certainly had more to say about the costs of care than mothers in two-earner families, in keeping with their lower levels of household income (Backett-Milburn et al., 2001).

It was interesting also to see the parents' perspectives on the policy issues relating to the quantity, quality and flexibility of child-care provision. There were few complaints about inadequate provision and no complaints about the nature of care provided by the carer being used. There are a number of possible explanations;

- those who are more satisfied may be more willing to give interviews;
- parents may not readily express dissatisfaction with child-care arrangements if it would make them feel guilty;
- if parents are very dissatisfied they are likely to change the arrangements, with the effect that, over time, there will be a trend towards satisfaction, rather than the reverse.

Which of these is predominant, and whether they all apply is difficult to determine. The finding of overall satisfaction with child-care arrangements is consistent with government survey evidence (Woodland et al., 2002) where 97 per cent of parents were satisfied with the child-care providers they had used in the week of the survey (76 per cent said it was very good and 21 per cent fairly good).

Parents did express problems about coordinating child care between different organisations that had different opening hours over the day and were geographically spread out (Skinner, 2003), as Box 2, page 66, describes. Dissatisfaction was also expressed about school schedules and rigid job schedules of mothers but probably even more so for fathers (Backett-Milburn et al., 2001; Reynolds et al., 2003; La Valle et al., 2002; Yeandle et al., 2002).

Informal child care
What becomes very clear from any in-depth research on parents and work is the enormous amount of unpaid and informal work going on caring for children in a day-to-day way (Mauthner et al., 2001; Backett-Milburn et al., 2001; Skinner, 2003; Reynolds et al., 2003). This predominance of informal child care in Britain has been evident as long as data have been collected about child-care usage.

In the mid-1990s at least two-thirds of children under five who received non-parental care were cared for by relatives or friends (Mooney et al., 2001). But the survey findings are only the part of a much larger picture. Until recently, survey questions have tended to focus on 'the main' type of child care used by working parents. In a few cases, the questions differentiate school term times from holiday care. But more in-depth studies show that even among the users of formal, paid provision, there is still a lot of use of informal care to fill the gaps and coordination of the seamless web that young children's care demands (Backett-Milburn, 2001; Mauthner et al., 2001; Skinner, 2003; Baines et al., forthcoming 2003). An example of the extreme juggling that takes place is described below from one of the programme's studies (see Box 2, page 66) (Skinner, 2003).

Although we do not have empirical evidence about the past to back this up, these sorts of informal child care are not particularly new. Defining child care from play is clearly a grey area. Children going to each other's houses to play has been a perennial practice over the generations. What may be new is the motivation for this practice, perhaps as a strategy to fill-in care gaps. They have to be arranged, often on a reciprocal basis, to cope with gaps and coordination in other non-parental care due to the schedules of paid work. As such, informal arrangements play a part in a complex web of relationships and social networks upon which the majority of employed parents rely.

Box 2: **Illustration of child-care arrangements of a two-earner family**

Source: summarised from Skinner (2003).

Family with two children. Child-care arrangements refer to time when children were age four and a baby. Father worked full-time. Mother worked full-time 37 hours per week.

The father takes the baby to full-time day nursery around 8 am and goes on to work by bike for 8.30. The mother walks the older child to school nursery and goes on to work by car to start shortly after 9 am on flexitime.

At lunchtime, the four year old has to be picked up at 11.45 am from school by the father, who was taking an early lunchbreak (11.30–12.30). The mother would take her lunch hour from 12.15 to 1.15 pm, which enabled her to go home, relieve her husband, collect the older child and take him to private nursery for 1 pm when they would take him for the afternoon session. Both children were cared for together in the afternoon at this private nursery until 5 pm. During the next term however, the older child changed from attending school nursery in the morning to attending in the afternoon session, which finished at 3 pm. To cover the gap in care for the older child from 3–5 pm a next door neighbour was paid to pick him up from school and keep him until the parents finished work.

The mother picks up both children from the private nursery four out of five evenings. The father had to pick up the children one night each week in order for the mother to work until 6 pm in order to fulfil her weekly hours quota and keep her ability to start after 9 am.

Some working parents continue to have a preference for informal, home-based care, despite the increase in formal provision. This is greater among low-income groups and, as this programme suggests, among many self-employed mothers (Bell and La Valle, 2003; Baines et al., forthcoming 2003). The link between low income and use of informal care led to the claim that the high cost of formal child care (and perhaps its accessibility) were the main drivers of this behaviour. But the research in this programme suggests this is a strong preference, related at least as much to attitudes and values as to costs. One gets the sense from the studies in this programme, that even with more money and higher earnings, many of these parents would make the same choice for informal care if it were possible. People who use informal child care from family and friends while they work do so feeling they can trust the carers, but not necessarily anyone else, to care for their child properly.

Provision of formal child care

The study of relocation (Green and Canny, 2003) and the comparison of caring in two local labour markets (Yeandle et al., 2002) found that more mobile communities need greater provision of formal child care to facilitate parents working. The latest government study by Woodland et al. (2002) of parents' demands for child care identified some form of unmet demand from 24 per cent of parents with a child under 14. However, parents said the experience of unmet demand occurred relatively infrequently. Given this intermittent and therefore low level of problem, the government needs to tread carefully in trying to expand provision. Pressing formal child-care on communities that rely on each other and their self-generated networks may not necessarily do them a service. Market relationships can rarely, if ever, match friendships and reciprocal community relationships for quality, persistence, fulfilment, flexibility and cost, especially in crises.

There is also the issue of child care at atypical times of day, given that increasing numbers of parents are working outside of the 9 to 5 day. La Valle et al. (2002) found that parents who worked more frequently at atypical times of day were more likely to use informal child-care provision, or share the child care between themselves. Statham and Mooney (2003) addressed the question of whether there was an unmet demand for child care at such times, by asking local agents for their views. The study reached the conclusions that there was a demand, though not a significant one. Twelve of the 114 of the EYDCPs (Early Years Development Childcare Partnerships) contacted thought there was 'significant' demand. Most of the rest thought there was some unmet demand, mainly for evenings and weekends, but not for overnight care. There was thought to be unmet demand for child care at times that varied from week to week.

Statham and Mooney's (2003) research also found that there were significant barriers to providing care at such times, as discussed in Chapter 1, but suggests that there may be ways of increasing the provision. However, these are not without problems that would need resolving. Groups of childminders may be able to work together, for example. However, this raises issues about the continuity and quality of care.

The study also suggested that, because of the small scale of the demand, and parents and providers not necessarily being able to identify each other, the appointment of local coordinators is needed who could help find or organise child-care providers who might agree to provide care at atypical times and match them to parents who wanted this provision. This would be an innovative partnership approach to try and address the information and coordination gap that occurs in this small market. However, one attempt at coordinating between employers to address childcare needs had failed in the East of England region (Dex and Scheibl, 2002). Another model of the way forward suggested by this study is to aim to integrate children's services, in the way used, for example, by the Neighbourhood Nurseries Initiative, the Sure Start programme and the proposals for Children's Centres. These too are partnership models between parents, local government and communities.

From April 2003 the government has allowed parents of children cared for at home to be eligible to claim the Childcare Tax Credit element of the new Working Tax Credit (the successor to the Working Families Tax Credit, or WFTC) to assist with the costs of child care. This *Home Childcarers Scheme* is only relevant to low income groups, or lone parents, as a way of helping them into work and making work pay compared with being reliant on benefits. It excludes care from nannies, therefore, presumably because high-income groups use them. It also has stringent conditions attached and only registered childminders, approved by Ofsted, will be eligible. This combination of conditions make it unlikely that many parents will benefit.

Innovative community nanny schemes of the sort described by Statham and Mooney (2003) will not be eligible for the tax-credit contributions from the Home Childcarers Scheme. Certainly, as expressed at its outset in April 2003, it is unlikely to add significantly, therefore, to the amount of provision of more flexible child care at atypical hours of work. Nor will it enable the majority of grandparents who care for grandchildren in the child's home, if they are paid, to have their payments eligible for tax relief.

Other family–community partnerships

Children's education

The study of mobile families relocated by their employer (Green and Canny, 2003) found that they needed help, possibly from their employer, especially with transferring their children from one local education authority to another (Green and Canny, 2003). The process of moving school-aged children to another part of the country has become much more fraught since school league tables and the stress on parental choice were introduced. It might appear that there is better information for those moving from one area to another, since league tables are published. However, mobile families are outsiders in the new area. Even if they can access the information, they are at a disadvantage to get places in 'the best' schools, as local competition is stiff, and housing is not necessarily available in the appropriate catchment area. It appears that employers have only just started to consider the issues relocation raises for families.

Loss of a mother's job and children's education stand out as the two most common problems relocating families have to face, at least, when their removal expenses have been met by the employer. Not surprisingly, families are more resistant to relocating than they used to be and more are willing to try commuting solutions as alternatives to relocation. However, this is not without its problems for families, who can be left with a lone parent in the week, and for a society that wants to cut down on road transport and pollution.

Social capital

Partnerships can also occur between parents and their wider families and friends. This is an area of relationships sometimes discussed under the heading of social capital. It is also commonly thought that links and networks between families have declined and lifestyles have become more privatised. Certainly, where records are available, it appears that fewer people engage in and are members of voluntary or religious organisations than used to be the case earlier this century (Putnam, 2002). Mothers going out to work has been one of the reasons cited for this decline, since mothers have transferred their time from unpaid voluntary work to paid market work. If voluntary organisations and informal social networks are considered to be the glue or cement holding societies together, these are potentially important developments.

What the projects in this programme have found is that informal and reciprocal networks still exist and are vital to the survival of the majority of working carers of older adults in Britain, parents of disabled children (Kagan et al., 1998) and other parents, as described above (Skinner, 2003; Phillips et al., 2002; Basu and Altinay, forthcoming 2003). All carers have been seen to create their own non-market partnerships with their wider family and friends. Carers of older adults, like those of young children, stressed the importance to them of friends and family in coping with work and care (Phillips et al., 2002). These links are the essence of building a sense of community.

These findings and the other information collected tangentially in these projects about communities pointed to their being a greater sense of community among the working class (Yeandle et al., 2002; Skinner, 2003; Backett-Milburn et al., 2001; Reynolds et al., 2003), lower mobility communities (Green and Canny, 2003; Yeandle et al., 2002; Reynolds et al., 2003), and in the three examples of rural areas (Mauthner et al., 2001). Conversely, the greater use of market care tended to be associated with higher mobility, more atomised and individualised parents, cut off from their roots and extended families (Yeandle et al., 2002; Reynolds et al., 2003). In some cases, and partly because of work, combined, in the case of London with long travel times to and from work, these families were also less in touch with old or new friends (Reynolds et al., 2003). Geographical mobility was found to break up families, taking parents from their children and from the grandparents in some cases (Green and Canny, 2003). Another group that clearly struggled and needed partnerships with their communities to a larger extent than other groups were the parents of disabled children (Kagan et al., 1998).

Studies in this programme showed that those parents living an individualised lifestyle were mostly still integrated into some informal networks of parents. It is the case, however, that geographical mobility as a result of employers' relocation policies, or promotions, and very long hours of work are factors that tend to destroy families' sense of, and integration into local communities. It is also the case that one cannot legislate for relationships of this kind. Nor can the growth of formal child-care provision, as useful as it can be, fully replace or compensate for social networks. These, as we saw earlier in this Chapter, are still vital to the operation of 'wrap-around' child care. However, it seems to be important that policy should avoid contributing to the destruction or demise of good relationships. Similarly, the low view of caring for children, whether it be done by parents or other unpaid carers needs challenging. Even parents, as we saw in Chapter 3 (from Reynolds et al., 2003), could express the view that staying at home to look after their children would be 'a waste of their time'.

Family business and ethnic minority communities

Family businesses are organisations where family life, work and sometimes home all overlap. This programme studied family businesses in five different ethnic minority groups (Basu and Altinay, forthcoming 2003), and included some family businesses in the two studies of the self-employed (Bell and La Valle, 2003; Baines et al., forthcoming 2003). Although working at home was not the focus of a particular study, since it was covered in the ESRC's Future of Work Programme, it was a relevant issue when the family businesses or self-employment also took place at home.

The study of 60 family businesses, among Indian, East African Asian, Bangladeshi, Pakistani and Turkish Cypriot ethnic minorities found that family relationships had been important to all of them, both at the start of the business and at the time of the study in 2000 (Basu and Altinay, forthcoming 2003). Fathers had taken the lead in all of the businesses examined, but women had helped in many, more so at the beginning than later in the businesses development. Some wives had worked in the business, some had worked outside the business to provide another income while it was in its early stages. These roles were still evident among a smaller number of wives in 2000, often 10 or more years after the start of the business. All had taken the major responsibility for caring for children and the family. The wider family had also been crucial in providing capital or loans to the business in its early days.

It was interesting to see a strong preference for the mother as child carer among the white majority in the two other studies of the self-employed (Baines et al., forthcoming 2003; Bell and La Valle, 2003), paralleled in the findings from the study of ethnic minority family businesses (Basu and Altinay, forthcoming 2003). It points to a link between self-employment or business owners and child-care preferences that cuts across ethnic origin.

The different ethnic communities had specialised in different types of business sector and this had, to some extent, influenced business growth and development, and the number and type of employees incorporated into the business. Geographical mobility among white communities in Britain was found to influence the extent to which they had access to wider family support; the same was found for ethnic minority businesses. East African Asian and Indian business owners placed greater reliance on their wider family's support, and their own community for employees, partly because it was available. Bangladeshi and Pakistani business owners placed greater reliance, as their businesses grew, on recruiting employees from outside their ethnic community, partly because they had fewer family and community members in the areas studied in the South East of England.

A concern about the family was expressed by all ethnic minority business owners. For these men, providing the family with a better life and standard of living was central to their aims. This was similar to the breadwinner role expressed by mainly white fathers in other studies. Mothers largely accepted the very long business hours that went with running a family business. A few of the women reflected on and showed awareness of some of the costs of the business on family life; the effect of the long hours on time with the children, and of living in the same premises as the business. But, overall, the business was seen as a valuable asset for the family, one for which the family needed to nurture, care and sacrifice.

In these ways, the business was in some cases more like a family itself. Certainly, the boundary between business and family was blurred for many of the ethnic minority family businesses studied. Whether the main aim was that the business was to provide for the family, or that the family was to provide for the business was not altogether clear. It was clear, however, that these ethnic minority entrepreneurs actively cultivated a sense of family and community. Similarly, many felt a responsibility to their wider family to offer support and employment, even when it was not always in the business's interest. Family and community were also closely related. East African Asians were more likely than other groups to involve family members to provide labour, capital and information at the start of the business as well as later. In part this reflected the greater extent of wider family resident in the UK than was the case for Indian, Pakistani or Bangladeshi business owners. East African Asians and Indians both had a higher propensity to delegate than other groups, and commonly employed professional managers. Turkish Cypriot business owners did not rely on family members at business start-up, to the same degree as the other groups, but did increase their involvement of family members over time. Turkish Cypriot owners were less likely to take on professional managers or non-family members, and neither were they interested in growing the business to the same extent as other groups.

Conclusions

This programme found many examples of partnerships between families and their communities. Partnerships, as these studies show, need not be formal or contractual, but can be informal and fluid networks and relationships. Families had supportive relationships with their employers, with unions, with formal and informal child-care providers, and with state services. Families' communities, therefore, were defined in a number of ways; by their area of residence, their networks, particularly for organising child care, their business or workplace, trade union, and ethnic group. Overall, many opportunities for partnerships were either being missed or not fully realised.

Geographical mobility was something that tended to weaken families' partnerships with their own wider family and their community of residence, and require greater partnership with either market or state services. Employers' relocation policies caused geographic mobility and affected the extent of family support and work–life balance for some families. Such policies, therefore, need to come under the government's work–life challenge policies umbrella. Similarly, the needs of parents of disabled children for partnerships with the community are considerable. Schools, hospitals and transport services for these groups all assume that mothers will be constantly available and not at work. There is a need to raise awareness about this group of working parents.

It was clear across these studies that formal child-care provision has increased more where demand has been greatest. Demand has been greatest where sense of community has been weakened through higher mobility. Mobility has tended to be higher among those with the highest social status and earnings. However, in the case of ethnic minorities, geographical mobility over very large distances has not weakened the sense of community or wider family to the same extent. It may even have increased it. Child care among the group of parents in the family businesses studied was largely provided by the mother, a fact that was common in the case of lower skilled parents in self-employment in the North East of England.

One challenge for future policy on child-care provision is to avoid weakening families' fragile social networks and reciprocal relations.

■ 5 Conclusions

At end of this programme of research we can consider some of the wider questions that are raised by families' involvement in paid work, questions that originally motivated this research programme.

Are families coping?

At the outset of this programme there was concern that families were under pressure in the new 24/7 economy of global competition, which affects workplaces, as well as families. We consider the issue of how families are coping. The research projects have tended to focus on two-earner couples, or employed lone parents, for reasons cited earlier.

The strategy of having two earners, one full-time, usually male, and one part-time, usually female, is one that appears to be effective in reducing risk and broadly provides the standard of living to which the majority of middle-income families aspire. Examining these families at a point in time, as these projects have tended to do, shows that they are managing to juggle work and family life, and are not in a state of total collapse. There are many tired parents and a large amount of dissatisfaction, particularly for mothers working weekends and fathers working shift patterns, weekends or long hours. Statistics suggesting that almost half of employed mothers would prefer to be at home caring for their own children if they could afford it show the reality of constraints. However, they also show that there are more underlying strains and pressures than might sometimes appear.

Where two-earner or even 1.5-earner families are most under pressure, and obviously on the edge of coping, is where they have heavy responsibility for caring for older adults, have a disabled child, or have the double caring loads for older adults and young children. Given the trend towards an older age of first childbirth for mothers, this relatively new pattern of double-care loads is likely to increase.

We did not set out to ask parents systematically what they want. When this was done, it was usually as the last question giving parents an opportunity to add their own agenda to that of the researchers. The answers are somewhat predictable. Everyone would like more money. In view of the pressures of the market place and our consumer society, it seems unlikely that families will ever reach totally satisfactory levels of income. Of course, it might be very nice if we lived in a world of unconstrained resources, but we do not. Earlier focus group studies found mothers voicing a strong preference for time-off for family emergencies. The fact that this was not often the main preference expressed in this programme's research projects may be related to different methods being used, or the knowledge that new legislation was in the pipeline at the time that would allow employees to take this time off unpaid.

However, some pointers to the areas where parents want most change did come out from the research.

- Mothers would like fathers to cut down long hours of work.
- Many mothers would prefer shorter hours of work, even giving up paid work altogether, if they could afford it.
- Mothers and fathers would prefer work for themselves and their partner that did not involve so much time on Sunday especially and weekends more generally.
- Both parents would like greater flexibility about work where they do not have it already.

There are, of course, a shrinking group of families who still rely on one, mainly male earner. This group is larger if viewed over the life-cycle rather than at the cross-sectional point in time, since many couples still have a period of time when one (usually male) partner works and the other (usually female) partner stays at home when children are born and are very young. We know relatively little about the group who persist with one earner for a longer period while their children are growing up and this is a gap that it would be useful to fill. Certainly, policy and benefit regimes have been largely ignoring this group.

Does work keep families out of poverty?

One of the government's main principles for addressing family issues has been that paid work is the route out of poverty for families. Clearly, most of the government's efforts have been directed at those families that do not have any paid work and earnings, that is, the no-earner households and lone parents on benefit. This programme did not focus specifically on families living in poverty, off benefit or making the transition from benefit to employment for reasons described at the outset. What we can see from this programme's research on dual-earner couples and lone parents who are working in low paid jobs (before the most recent 2003 Budget changes that were aimed at helping the latter group financially) is that they were managing to keep out of poverty, but that, for some, it is a difficult job.

Many faced issues related to the cost and organisation of child care since their budgets are finely tuned, with little slack. The 2003 Budget changes will help with household finances for some of these parents. However, survey work suggested that many mothers' preferences run counter to the direction government policy is trying to encourage, since they would prefer to do less rather than more work while their children are young.

It should also be noted, however, that materialism and consumerism are strong drivers of parent's and children's values and aspirations, at both middle and low income levels. Many parents believe that they are not giving their children the best start in life if they cannot buy them the latest toys or clothes. While this is a strong motivator for parents, including the employed lone parents, to have paid jobs, there is also a sense in which it is an unreachable goal. The demand keeps on, fuelled by advertising and peer pressure, and is never fulfilled. In this sense, an escape from feelings of relative disadvantage rarely will be achieved. The government needs to consider, alongside its targets to eliminate child poverty, the way advertising to children may be helping to nullify any feelings of improvement from additional income in poor families.

The other problem with the government's seemingly worthy target for families is that it signals that only paid work is important. This is unfortunate, and far from ideal since it reinforces the low value placed on unpaid work and care. Even childminders who are paid to care expressed that this low valuation affected them and their morale. There is also an overlapping implication; that paid child care is better than parental care. However, unpaid child care is preferred by many parents. It helps to create a sense of community and is more flexible and cheaper, for parents and the public purse. Policy should try to avoid destructive effects on parents' sense of community.

Is child care still a problem for working families?

Since the 1980s child-care provision has increased substantially in Britain, and we now have the oversight and activity of a National Child Care Strategy. More families are using paid formal child care than used to be the case and, clearly, provision has increased. Britain used to lag way behind other European countries in the extent of formal child-care provision, although this is not the case any more. However, the cost of child care may still be high in Britain relative to some other European countries.

It was right to give the development of formal provision priority and to address some clear gaps. We need to consider at what point the situation is satisfactory for parents who want to work. Again, these studies were not trying to evaluate total demand for child care. The government department concerned is currently doing this at yearly intervals (La Valle et al., 2000; Woodland et al., 2002). Nonetheless, qualitative interviews with parents and this survey work did uncover how parents use and feel about child-care provision.

The school holidays and after school are still the most difficult times, although unanticipated changes to the school schedule also pose problems. Whilst after-school and holiday clubs have increased, they cost money and this is beyond the budget of some parents, especially those on low incomes. Some parents who work atypical hours can arrange child care around their schedules, but others find it a serious problem where shifts and days worked vary.

The tall order for policy is that additional child-care places would be helpful in some areas if the following points were considered:

- They should be flexible in terms of the start and finish times.
- It could be possible to have some variation in the days used by parents from week to week without payment for off days.
- There could be increases in low cost but same quality school-holiday clubs that varied each holiday.
- There was better supervision and bullying was addressed in school-holiday clubs.
- Schools could organise care for children of working parents to cover training days and other irregular gaps in the school timetable.

- More attention could be given to the coordination and associated geography problems parents face, particularly when their children are starting school and there is more than one child in the family. These arise because of rigid schedules in child care or early education providers that do not overlap with the opening hours of other child-care facilities, and there is little provision for getting a child from one provider to another at either midday or the end of the day. Many of these problems could be addressed if there were more combined child-care centres based around early education providers.

However, some parents, especially those on low incomes, do not want to feel they are putting their children into seamless child-care and never seeing them. So it is not simply a matter of increasing child-care places. The implications for policy of the continuing preference for informal child-care are hardly being addressed. This may be a controversial and disputed conclusion in some quarters. The strong preference for informal care suggests that setting the target at being able to provide places for all children (in the age group) in all areas is likely to be far too high, leading to excess supply – even if it were possible to generate all the places. Market solutions, often favoured in Britain, have already been finding the demand is too low in some areas. The three rural areas in one of this programme's studies found it difficult to enrol critical levels of children for a viable business (Mauthner, et al., 2001). The same result has emerged for care at atypical times of day (Mooney and Statham, 2003).

Arguing that parents in rural areas or those working at atypical times should have additional subsidy for child-care places, in an attempt to increase demand for them would be problematic, controversial and raise more equity issues. In addition, this would aim to attract parents to use formal child-care; many of these parents are currently satisfied with their more informal arrangements with friends and relatives. We, as a society, also need to consider whether we want to help pay for child care for parents to be working evenings and weekends. It would not be difficult to argue that it would be more effective to give these parents the money. Also, if new child-care services cannot generate sufficient demand to create a viable business, there may need to be greater scrutiny of their business plans at the outset and more effective and inclusive business support agencies than are currently in place. Policy needs to tread carefully in this area, to avoid wasting resources and patronising low-income groups.

Policy also needs to consider the equity issues when devising child-care subsidies and assistance. There is a measure of inequity if lone (or other) parents and low-income groups are given financial assistance for child-care expenses if they pay for formal child care, but that those who prefer informal care for their children do not receive any benefits.

This programme identified a number of barriers to extending the formal child-care workforce: its quantity, flexibility and quality. Grandparents and other relatives are often providing the informal care and, as such, constitute part of the informal child-care workforce. Policies being discussed about increasing the retirement age, as a way of easing the problem of funding pensions, could end up reducing this labour force of child carers (and carers for even older adults) in future.

Is work or family the central life-interest for parents?

The stereotyped view of mothers and fathers has been that work is the central life-interest of fathers and men in general, whereas family is the central life-interest of mothers. The research in this programme challenges that dichotomy for the majority of working parents. Both fathers and mothers expressed different and more complex views and values about work and family life. The various projects have covered a range of families, although some views, possibly those that fit the stereotypes, may be under-represented in these research projects.

The main message coming across from these broadly middle-income 1.5-earner households is that family comes first for both mothers and fathers. However, for both parents, earning income to support the family is also seen as central to providing for the family and its security. Fathers had the added sense of responsibility of being the breadwinner over mothers, who were happy to see their financial contribution as a component share of family providing. However, the majority of fathers asked were pleased that mothers were adding a component to household income.

Underneath these views there was a strong value, for many, that material goods and standard of living was very important. A few rural *downshifters* were trying to break out of such values, to make their lives revolve around different priorities. The majority who wanted an acceptable standard of living did also value good relationships, but they were clearly prepared to prioritise in order to achieve the standard of living they wanted. The order of priorities, for those who could not have it all, were children first, spouse and self second, and wider family and friends third. Time pressures meant that many never got beyond their first priority. It is somewhat ironic that the same parents who were saying children come first had also largely bought into the view that only paid work has value, implying a low value on child care, done either by themselves, or by others.

This prioritising of children also uncovers the sort of thinking and processes that lie behind statistical correlations of mothers' full-time employment with divorce rates among couples. Putting couples' needs for each other second and after children, and finding that rarely is there time to attend and nurture the lower ranking relationships when both partners work, can leave a couple's relationship starved of (time) investment. It is a larger gap in cases where long hours are worked or there are two atypical working schedules, a gap that can be filled with disillusion about marriage and the value of partnerships for individual parents. This is in addition to tiredness. Interestingly, it may, in part, be the same underlying causes that explain why a growing number of couples, in wanting to give priority to their relationship with their partner and work, opt for childless unions (McAllister and Clarke, 1998). Ironically, dual-earner couples also had a more intense focus on their relationship with each other, since wider family and friends are even lower in the priority and time budgeted list.

Are social networks disintegrating?

While parents' time to engage in maintaining relationships with the wider family, friends and spouses – and voluntary activities – has undoubtedly been squeezed by paid work, some networks have grown. One network has become more central and vital, especially to mothers who work: this is the child-care network. Many low-income mothers rely on family and friends for child care. Even those in middle-income groups who use formal paid care, rely on informal care provided by family and friends to gain added flexibility around their core hours of formal paid care.

The low-income parents have better networks than higher-income families in this respect. This is partly because low-income workers are also less mobile and more likely, therefore, to have wider family in the vicinity and longer friendships to call upon. But parents living in rural areas and lone parents were also better integrated into networks of relationships that were happy to provide, in some cases, reciprocal child care.

Some commentators think of social networks as providers of opportunities, for example jobs, in the case of the unemployed, or better jobs, in the case of the employed. The networks that are used to provide informal child care are not those of the well connected, but are survival networks of lower income parents juggling competing demands and trying to raise their standard of living at the margins. They are networks nonetheless, and clearly valued by those who use them. Whether such relationships continue after young children have grown old enough to look after themselves remains to be researched.

Has labour market deregulation changed the profile of employment and workplaces?

This programme was launched against the background legacy of extensive labour market deregulation and a large decline in trade union membership and coverage in workplaces. The research in this programme has highlighted the large participation by mothers and fathers in jobs with atypical hours or times of day. The decline in unions probably paved the way for a faster movement away from standard hours and contracts than might otherwise have occurred, although clearly, pressures have been pushing employers in this direction for some time. Many families expressed feelings of insecurity about men's jobs, especially in rural areas and in the North East.

However, it is not all doom and gloom from the employees' perspective. Working at times outside of the normal 9 to 5 day and part-time has suited many families, especially mothers. Mothers have seen this as a good way of combining some paid work and family life. Even though the jobs may not be very glamorous, they are appreciated for their social contacts and additional cash. In a few cases, researchers were surprised by the amounts of autonomy and pride workers felt about what others might think of as fairly low-skilled or menial jobs. This was particularly the case for employees working in the public services, where an ethos of caring could make jobs seem worthwhile. However, the 24/7 economy's spread into Sunday and the weekend has not met with the same positive response.

Parents, as we have seen, are over-represented in the jobs in the 24/7 workplace. For some, this has given new opportunities for paid work that suited their preference to share care of their own children with their partner. For other parent employees, work and child care at atypical times of day has been a problem. In the past, employment outside of 9 to 5 on weekdays attracted higher rates of pay, which could have been a way employers made a contribution towards the costs of replacement child care for those who needed it. Instead, commentators now advocate the general tax payer be responsible for providing subsidised child-care places at atypical times of day, to support the low-wage economy, as well as lower priced goods and services.

One of the effects of deregulation, therefore, may be to draw the state into increasing support to sustain the low-wage sector. This raises an issue about the state's role in supporting families versus parental autonomy, which is part of a much larger debate raised by the approach to parenting policy under the current government (see Henricson, 2003). At the same time, as noted above, some employers have been providing more flexible working arrangements that suit parents' needs and preferences. Unions have been involved in this provision where they were still in evidence, although there has also been a growth in such provisions in workplaces where high commitment management practices were being used and unions were absent.

Although many part-time jobs held by women have been low-paid and low-skilled jobs, where employers have allowed their employees to change to more flexible working arrangements, these are not typical 'junk jobs'. They can be part of the newer 'knowledge work' economy. It is clear that parents do not feel that good quality flexible working arrangements for both mothers and, especially, fathers has developed far enough.

Do we need more regulation?

As mentioned at the outset, employers and labour markets have experienced large amounts of new regulation and legislation since 1997, aimed at helping families and those on low incomes. The April 2003 Budget introduced a range of new measures (see Box 1, page 7). The government will undoubtedly be intending to evaluate all of its new programmes and regulations in a way that this programme could not. We have heard from small businesses, as do all researchers of this sector, that they do not want any further regulation imposed on them. Certainly, just in terms of letting things settle and be evaluated, the case for further regulation is not strong. It was clear that there was much confusion among employers about the labels of the various legislative provisions, for example parental versus paternity leave, to the extent that a simpler umbrella term might be of benefit.

The aim here was to consider whether this programme has uncovered problems, the solution to which is further regulation. Regulation could be appropriate if there were serious third party or societal costs, or public interest issues that employers have a disincentive to address or have an incentive to make worse. One caveat about the introduction of more legislation is that this programme's studies have reaffirmed that many employment relationships and flexibility rest on a foundation of trust. Perhaps they even work best when based on trust and good relationships in the workplace. A rights-based approach embedded in much legislation can be combined with the development of trust-based practices, but may undermine trust; this is an issue that cannot be developed further in this report, but that requires serious consideration.

In Britain in April 2003 higher benefits were introduced for children or the vast majority of families and, through the route of tax credits, additionally to those on lower incomes. Greater contributions towards the child-care expenses of lone parent and very low-income families were also introduced as Child Care Tax Credits. These are aimed at making it pay for families to be in work, rather than out of work. However, parents who stay at home to care for their own children are also to benefit from the increased benefits for children. Although the amounts in question do not go very far to reverse the inequities embedded in tax system changes since the 1980s, which penalised one-earner couples, it is at least a start.

Child-care provision is still increasing through the National Child Care Strategy and Sure Start scheme, and pilot schemes to explore providing 'wrap-around' care are also being developed. These, along with combined family centres, may address some of the remaining pockets of child-care problems.

The proposals put forward by the Work and Parents Taskforce available from April 2003, are in tune with the policy implications advocated by at least one project in this programme. Parents have been expressing the desire for greater flexibility in their working arrangements. In this sense, government is already taking up one area of further regulation. It is, however, aiming to be *light-touch* legislation, which puts the minimum of burden on employers, small employers included. The evidence of this programme is that this approach may even lead to benefits for employers. It could benefit employers even more were this approach to be extended to any employee to apply, not just parents of a child under six years, as at present.

There are two other areas where parents' responses indicate the need to consider the issue of further regulation; long hours of work, and Sunday and weekend work. In the case of long hours of work, the Working Time Directive is acknowledged by many to have allowed too many opt outs. Tightening-up of the regulations that restrict weekly working hours seems a good idea. However, even the existing 48 hours per week limit puts parents' involvement in family life in the problem zone. If, as is expected, the implementation of the Work and Parents Taskforce proposals provide for parents to request flexibility and reduced hours, then it should be possible to provide an opportunity for those who choose time with the family over additional earnings to be able to exercise their choice.

On the issue of Sunday working, pressures are being exerted to further deregulate and extend shop-opening hours on Sundays from the current limit of six hours opening. Ironically, before the last deregulation of Sunday working hours, it was argued, among other things, that working mothers needed longer opening hours in order to do their shopping. However, the large extent to which parents have been drawn into working at weekends, not by preference, now suggests that they do not see themselves as net beneficiaries of this earlier extension.

Parents' responses in this programme suggest there is a need to limit any further increases in Sunday working for parents, and even to pull back from the current position. Certainly, there needs to be some review of parents' involvement in weekend working and proposals need to be drawn up that would ensure time off at weekends for parents to overlap with their school-aged children, on a regular basis.

With these few exceptions or clarifications, the need for further legislation is not currently pressing. However, as the recent review of parenting policy by Henricson (2003) shows, there is a strong case for injecting more social cohesion into British family policy for the benefit of parents. Of course, much of our newer legislation in the area of family policy has had its origins in Europe, coming to Britain through European directives. Britain has taken up some of these challenges (for example paid paternity leave) at a slower pace than other European countries. This route of policy will undoubtedly bring pressures for new regulation in future. The problems of funding pensions for the population is an issue exercising all advanced industrialised countries. This is likely to bring new pressures to work longer, and have fewer or shorter breaks from employment.

Are workplaces responding to the changing workforce?

Workplaces are responding to the changing workforce and to family pressures. Some are leading the field in providing greater flexibility in their working arrangements; these are both small and large employers. Others are resistant to any change, not just changes in working patterns but including, in some cases, adapting to new technology. Clearly, some of the changes introduced are more for the benefit of employers than for employees and their families, and some are window-dressing, leaving the main workplace culture one that is anti-flexibility. However, even in the cases of change for the employers' benefit, some, but not all, employees have found it suited their needs.

Changes in young people's preferences about work, and the demographics that predict an intensification in the competition for talent all point to the future becoming more flexible than the present for some workers. However, the pervasive long-hours cultures in some workplaces remains as an issue that needs addressing. Predominantly male workplaces may need particular inducements to adopt more flexible working arrangements. Employers' relocation policies also need a detailed internal review of their rationale, costs and benefits, as well as a societal audit of their costs and benefits.

Workplace carers of older adults face a Cinderella of organisation work–life policies. This is an area of low levels of development, where companies in 2001 appear only just beginning to think about the issues. Even where they have policies in place they are rarely used, line managers preferring to use existing policies they understand, but with the effect that carers do not get time off or the opportunity to rest or recoup from heavy caring duties. The National Strategy for Carers should certainly take time to consider, in partnership with the Work–Life Balance campaign and human resource practitioners, how workplace policy could improve in this area and have, as a minimum, guidelines and recommendations.

References

Airy, C., Hales, J., Hamilton, R., Korovessis, C., McKenna, A. and Purdon, S. (1999) *The Workplace–employee relations survey (WERS) 1997–98 technical report*, London: National Centre for Social Research.

Akerlof, G. (1998) 'Men without children', *Economic Journal*, 108, 257–309.

Backett-Milburn, K., Cunningham-Burley, S. and Kemmer, D. (2001) *Caring and providing: Lone and partnered working mothers in Scotland*, Bristol: The Policy Press/Joseph Rowntree Foundation, *Family and Work series.*

Bailyn, L. (1993) *Breaking the mold: Women, men and time in the new corporate world*, New York: Maxwell Macmillan.

Baines, S., Wheelock, J. and Gelder, U. (forthcoming 2003) *Riding the rollercoaster: Family life and self employment*, Bristol: The Policy Press/Joseph Rowntree Foundation, *Family and Work series.*

Basu, A. and Altinay, E. (forthcoming 2003) *Family and work in ethnic minority businesses*, Bristol: The Policy Press/Joseph Rowntree Foundation, *Family and Work series.*

Beck, U. (1992) *The risk society: Towards a new modernity*, London: Sage Publications.

Bell, A. and La Valle, I. (2003) *Combining self-employment and family life*, Bristol: The Policy Press/Joseph Rowntree Foundation, *Family and work series.*

Bevan, S., Dench, S., Tamkin, P. and Cummings, J. (1999) *Family-friendly employment: The business case*, London: Department for Education and Employment, Research Report RR136.

Bond, S., Hyman, J., Summers, J. and Wise, S. (2002) *Family-friendly working? Putting policy into practice*, Bristol: The Policy Press/Joseph Rowntree Foundation, *Family and Work series.*

Brannen, J., Lewis, S., Nilsen, A. and Smithson, J. (2001*) Young Europeans, work and family life: Futures in transition*, London: Routledge.

Burchell, B., Day, D., Hudson, M., Lapido, D., Mankelow, R., Nolan, J., Reed, H., Witshert, I.C. and Wilkinson, F. (1999) *Job insecurity and work intensification: Flexibility and the changing boundaries of work*, York: YPS/Joseph Rowntree Foundation.

Burgess, S. and Rees, H. (1996) 'Job tenure in Britain 1975–92', *Economic Journal*, 106(435), 334–44.

Burghes, L., Clarke, L. and Cronin, N. (1997) *Fathers and fatherhood in Britain*, London: Family Policy Studies Centre/Joseph Rowntree Foundation, Occasional Paper 23.

Crompton, R., Dennett, J. and Wigfield, A. (forthcoming 2003) *Organisations, careers and caring*, Bristol: The Policy Press/Joseph Rowntree Foundation, *Family and Work series.*

Dench, G. (1996) *The place of men in changing family cultures*, London: Institute of Community Studies.

Dex, S. (ed.) (1999) *Families and the labour market: Trends, pressures and policies*, London: Family Policy Studies Centre/Joseph Rowntree Foundation.

Dex, S. and Scheibl, F. (1999) 'The business case for family-friendly policies' *Journal of General Management*, 24(4), 22–37.

Dex, S. and Scheibl, F. (2002) *SMEs and flexible working arrangements*, Bristol: The Policy Press/Joseph Rowntree Foundation, *Family and Work series*.

Dex, S. and Smith, C. (2002) *The nature and pattern of family-friendly employment policies in Britain*, Bristol: The Policy Press/Joseph Rowntree Foundation, *Family and Work series*.

Dex, S., Smith, C. and Winter, S. (2001) 'Effects of family-friendly policies on business performance', Judge Institute Research Paper series WP 22/01, University of Cambridge.

DfEE (Department for Education and Employment) (1998) *Meeting the childcare challenge*, CM 3959, London: Department for Education and Employment.

DfES (Department for Education and Skills) (2001) *Childcare and atypical work*, London: Department for Education and Skills, EYDCP Report 42.

DH (Department of Health) (1999) *Caring about carers: A national strategy for carers*, London: HMSO.

DTI (Department of Trade and Industry) (2000) *Work and parents: Competitiveness and choice. A Green Paper*, London: Department of Trade and Industry.

Dunscombe, J. and Marsden, D. (1993) 'Love and intimacy: The gender division of emotion and emotion work', *Sociology*, 27(2), 221–42.

Edwards, J.R. and Rothbard, N.P. (2000) 'Mechanisms linking work and family: Clarifying the relationship between work and family constructs', *Academy of Management Review*, 25(1), 178–99.

Ermisch, J. and Francesconi, M. (1997) *Family matters*, Colchester: ESRC Research Centre on Micro-social Change, University of Essex, Working Paper 97-1.

Ermisch, J. and Franscesconi, M. (2001) *The effects of parents' employment on children's lives*, Bristol: The Policy Press/Joseph Rowntree Foundation, *Family and Work series*.

Farrington, D. (2000) 'Psychosocial predictors of adult antisocial personality and adult convictions', *Behavioral Sciences and the Law*, 18, 605–22.

Furedi, F. (2001) *Paranoid parenting: Abandon your anxieties and be a good parent*, London: Allen Lane.

Green, A.E. and Canny, A. (2003) *Geographical mobility: Family impacts*, Bristol: The Policy Press/Joseph Rowntree Foundation, *Family and Work series*.

Harkness, S., Machin, S. and Waldfogel, J. (1995) 'Evaluating the pin money hypothesis: The relationship between women's labour market activity, family income and poverty in Britain', London: STICERD, London School of Economics, Welfare State Programme 108.

Hatter, W., Vinter, L. and Williams, R. (2002) *Dads on dads: Needs and expectations at home and work*, Manchester: Equal Opportunities Commission, Research Discussion Series.

Haveman, R. and Wolfe, B. (1995) 'The determinants of children's attainment: A review of methods and findings', *Journal of Economic Literature*, 33: 1829–78.

Henricson, C. (2003) *Government and parenting: Is there a case for a policy review and a parents' code?* York: Joseph Rowntree Foundation.

Hill, R. and Dex, S. (1999) 'The business and family consequences of deregulating Sunday trading in Britain', Cambridge: Judge Institute of Management, University of Cambridge, Research Paper WP34-99.

Hochschild, A. (1990) *The second shift: The revolution at home*, London: Piaktus.

Hogarth, T., Hasluck, C., Pierre, G., Winterbotham, M. and Vivian, D. (2001) *Work–life balance 2000: Baseline study of work–life balance practices in Great Britain*, Warwick: Institute for Employment Research, Warwick University.

Holtermann, S., Brannen, J., Moss, J. and Owen, C. (1999) *Lone parents and the labour market: Results from the 1997 Labour Force Survey and Review of Research*, London: Employment Service Research and Development Report, ESR23.

Houston, D. and Marks, G. (2000) *Employment choices for mothers of pre-school children: A psychological perspective*. ESRC End of Award Report L212252019, available at <http://www.regard.ac.uk/regard/home/index_html?>. Visited 17 June 2003.

Houston, D. and Waumsley, J. (forthcoming 2003) *Attitudes to flexible working and family life*, Bristol: The Policy Press/Joseph Rowntree Foundation, *Family and Work series*.

Kagan, C., Lewis, S. and Heaton, P. (1998) *Caring to work: Accounts of working parents of disabled children*, London: Family Policy Studies Centre/Joseph Rowntree Foundation.

Kiernan, K. (1996) 'Lone motherhood, employment and outcomes for children', *International Journal of Law, Policy and the Family*, 10, 233–49.

La Valle, I., Finch, S., Nove, A. and Lewin, C. (2000) *Parents' demand for child care*, London: DfEE Research Report, 176.

La Valle, I., Arthur, S., Millward, C., Scott, J. and Claydon, M. (2002) *Happy families? Atypical work and its influence on family life*, Bristol: The Policy Press/Joseph Rowntree Foundation, *Family and Work series*.

Martin, J. and Roberts, C. (1984) *Women and employment: A life time perspective*, Department of Employment/Office of Population Censuses and Surveys, London: The Stationery Office.

Mauthner, N., McKee, L. and Strell, M. (2001) *Work and family life in rural communities*, York: YPS/Joseph Rowntree Foundation.

McAllister, F. and Clarke, L. (1998) *Choosing childlessness*, London: Family Policy Studies Centre/Joseph Rowntree Foundation.

Mooney, A., Knight, A., Moss, P. and Owen, C. (2001) *Who cares? Childminding in the 1990s*, London: Family Policy Studies Centre/Joseph Rowntree Foundation, *Family and Work series*.

Osgood, J. (2003) *Developing the business skills of childcare professionals: An evaluation of the Business Support Programme,* London: DfES, Research Report RR421.

Phillips, J., Bernard, M. and Chittenden, M. (2002) *Juggling work and care: The experiences of working carers of older adults,* Bristol: The Policy Press/Joseph Rowntree Foundation, *Family and Work series.*

Princess Royal Trust for Carers (1995) *Carers in employment: A report on the development of policies to support carers at work,* Glasgow: Princess Royal Trust for Carers with BT.

Putnam, R. (2002) *Democracies in flux: The evolution of social capital in contemporary society,* New York: Oxford University Press.

Reynolds, T., Callendar, C. and Edwards, R. (2003) *Caring and counting: The impact of mothers' employment on family relationships,* Bristol: The Policy Press/Joseph Rowntree Foundation, *Family and Work series.*

Rolfe, H., Metcalf, H., Anderson, T. and Meadows, P. (2003) *Recruitment and retention of childcare, early years and play workers: Research study,* London: DfES, Research Report RR409.

Skinner, C. (2003) *Running around in circles: Co-ordinating childcare, education and work,* Bristol: The Policy Press/Joseph Rowntree Foundation, *Family and Work series.*

Statham, J. and Mooney, A. (2003) *Around the clock: Childcare services at atypical times,* Bristol: The Policy Press/Joseph Rowntree Foundation, *Family and Work series.*

TUC Changing Times website: <www.tuc.org.uk/theme/index.cfm?theme=changingtimes&startrow=1&endrow=3>. Visited 17 June 2003.

Warin, J., Solomon, Y., Lewis, C. and Langford, W. (1999) *Fathers, work and family life,* London: Family Policy Studies Centre/Joseph Rowntree Foundation.

Woodland, S., Miller, M. and Tipping, S. (2002) *Repeat study of parents' demand for childcare,* London: DfES, Research Report No. 348.

Yeandle, S., Crompton, R., Wigfield, A. and Dennett, J. (2002) *Employed carers and family-friendly employment policies,* Bristol: The Policy Press/Joseph Rowntree Foundation, *Family and Work series.*

Appendix ■

Projects and publications in the JRF Work and Family Life research programme

> Note: *Findings* mentioned below are published by the Joseph Rowntree Foundation. They can be downloaded at www.jrf.org.uk (or call 01904 615905). All reports are published in the Family and Work series by The Policy Press in association with JRF and are available from Marston Book Services on 01235 465500 (p&p £2.75 plus 50p for every extra publication).

The impact on families of changing patterns of paid work

1 The effect of parents' working on children's achievements

Publications

John Ermisch and Marco Francesconi (March 2001) 'The effect of parents' employment on outcomes for children', Findings No. 321

John Ermisch and Marco Francesconi (2001) *The effects of parents' employment on children's lives* (£10.95 ISBN 1 901455 60 2)

Research team
John Ermisch
University of Essex
Institute for Social and Economic Research
Wivenhoe Park
Colchester CO4 3SQ
Tel: 01206 872335   Email: ermij@essex.ac.uk

Marco Francesconi
University of Essex
Institute for Social and Economic Research
Tel: 01206 873534   Email: mfranc@essex.ac.uk

Project summary
The father's and mother's employment and type of job influence both the income coming into the family and parental time devoted to their children's development, and they also may help form role models for children. Thus, parents' working patterns may affect their children's educational achievements, economic success and health as adults. The aim of this research

was to examine whether a number of outcomes during young adulthood – educational attainments, unemployment, age at leaving home, health and early childbearing – are associated with parents' employment patterns during childhood. Measurement of these associations must be put in the context of other family influences on these outcomes. Thus, the project also considered whether these outcomes are associated with experience of life in a single parent family during childhood, with family income and with other aspects of family background (e.g. number of siblings and parents' education). A secondary analysis of data from a special sample selected using the first six waves of the British Household Panel Study was carried out. The sample consisted of individuals born between 1965 and 1980 who co-resided with their mothers for at least one year during six waves (1991–96) of the panel study. A particular feature of the analysis was that it used differences between siblings to control for aspects of family life that cannot usually be measured.

2 Caring and providing: A comparative study of the perceptions and experiences of lone and partnered mothers combining parenting and paid work

Publications

Kathryn Backett-Milburn, Sarah Cunningham-Burley and Debbie Kemmer (March 2001) 'Experiences of lone and partnered working mothers in Scotland', Findings No. 381

Kathryn Backett-Milburn, Sarah Cunningham-Burley and Debbie Kemmer (2001) *Caring and providing: Lone and partnered working mothers in Scotland* (£12.95 ISBN 1 901455 61 0)

Research team
Kathryn Backett-Milburn
University of Edinburgh
Medical School, Teviot Place
Edinburgh EH8 9AG
Tel: 0131 650 6197   Email: k.milburn@ed.ac.uk

Sarah Cunningham-Burley
University of Edinburgh
Medical School
Email: Sarah.C.Burley@ed.ac.uk

Project summary
In the UK, there is growing emphasis on work as a route out of poverty for lone and low-income parents. This is coupled with an increasing concern about parenting skills and a reaffirmation of parental responsibilities. This qualitative research project, carried out over a 20 month period (1998–2000), explored the views and realities of a sample of 30 working mothers, both lone and partnered, with children of primary school age. Their occupations, and those of their partners, fell into the Registrar General's categorisations iii, iv and v – in other words, non-professional/non-managerial occupations. Two in-depth interviews were conducted with each mother, followed by six focus group interviews with a range of people

working in policy and practice-related areas. The project examined the day to day challenges and practical decision-making involved in combining parenting and paid work and how these may change over time. It also explored the social contexts and cultural values around parenting in the context of the labour market, and documented the range of childcare arrangements used by mothers at different times. In order to develop policy that will anticipate and support all working mothers in the future, it was important to explore women's own accounts and understandings of combining work and parenting.

3 Changing work–family configurations: An ethnography of three rural communities

Publications

Natasha Mauthner, Lorna McKee and Monika Strell (September 2001) 'Work and family life in rural communities', Findings No. 971

Natasha Mauthner, Lorna McKee and Monika Strell (2001) *Work and family life in rural communities* (£14.95 ISBN 1 84263 054 7)

Research team
Natasha Mauthner
University of Aberdeen, Management Studies
Aberdeen Business School
Edward Wright Building
Aberdeen AB24 3QY
Tel: 01224 272712   Email: n.mauthner@abdn.ac.uk

Lorna McKee
University of Aberdeen, Management Studies
Aberdeen Business School
Tel: 01224 272712   Email: l.mckee@abdn.ac.uk

Project summary
This study brought together two issues that are at the forefront of current research and policy agendas, but which have largely been treated separately: the reconciliation of work and family life, and the social and economic changes affecting rural areas. The study explored how families living in rural communities combine work and family responsibilities against the backdrop of changes in rural economies, the nature of work, and family life. The study was based in and around three contrasting rural communities in North East Scotland, Northumberland and South West Scotland. An ethnographic approach was adopted involving two-month stays and participant observation within each community. The key focus of the study was on 52 two-parent households, from occupationally and socially diverse backgrounds. All households had at least one earner and one child aged 12 or under. Additional fieldwork was conducted with community figures and local employers. The study investigated household experiences of living and working within a rural community. It explored the diverse and evolving ways in which households combine breadwinning and

caring activities; and it examined the structural, ideological, social, interpersonal and individual factors that influence these work–family configurations.

4(a) Who cares? Childminding in the 1990s

Publications
See project 4(b) below.

Research team
Peter Moss
Thomas Coram Research Unit
Institute of Education
27/28 Woburn Square
London WC1H 0AA
Tel: 0207 612 6954   Email: tcru6@ioe.ac.uk.

Ann Mooney
Thomas Coram Research Unit
Tel: 0207 612 6948   Email: tetcaam@ioe.ac.uk.

Charlie Owen
Thomas Coram Research Unit
Tel: 0207 612 6942   Email: c.owen@ioe.ac.uk

Project summary
Childminding is both an important form of childcare and a major source of employment for women, often when they are mothers themselves. Childminding has received relatively little research attention since the mid-1980s: yet since then there have been major changes, both in the numbers of childminders and the context in which they operate, with a rapid increase in employed parents and a new regulatory framework following the 1989 Children Act. This project studied childminders as a distinctive group within the total childcare workforce, including their past employment histories, their current employment situation and their views about and commitment to their work. It also examined the contribution of childminding to the overall provision of child-care for children with employed parents. The research lasted 18 months, starting in January 1999. It consisted of three stages: secondary analysis of the Family Resources Survey, to examine the contemporary role of childminding in the provision of childcare; a large-scale survey involving a nationally representative sample of 1,050 childminders drawn from eight English authorities; and case studies of small numbers of new and well-established childminders, as well as childminders who had recently left the occupation.

4(b) Who cares? Childminding in the 1990s (follow-on)

Publications
Ann Mooney, Abigail Knight, Peter Moss and Charlie Owen (May 2001) 'Childminding in the 1990s', Findings No. 511

Ann Mooney, Abigail Knight, Peter Moss and Charlie Owen (2001) *Who cares? Childminding in the 1990s* (£13.95 ISBN 1 901455 62 9)

Research team
See 4(a) above.

Project summary
The project was an extension of the previous study of childminding as an occupation (4a), and investigated why the number of registered childminders, as recorded in official statistics, had fallen substantially in recent years. The investigation involved three parts. First, official statistics for childminding, as well as other types of childcare and early years education, were analysed for 1996–1999 at a local authority level, to examine the uniformity of the fall over time and across authorities, and whether there is any relationship between changes in the numbers of childminders and in places available in other forms of provision. Second, visits were made to ten local authorities, to explore with staff working with childminders what might be the reasons for falling numbers in their area. Third, work was undertaken with national and regional staff from the National Childminding Association, to seek their perspectives and explanations concerning recent trends.

5 The impact of mothers' increasing labour market participation on family relationships

Publications
Tracey Reynolds, Claire Callender and Rosalind Edwards (July 2003) 'The impact of mothers' employment on family relationships', Findings No. 773

Tracey Reynolds, Claire Callender and Rosalind Edwards (2003) *Caring and counting: The impact of mothers' employment on family relationships* (£14.95 ISBN 1 86134 534 8)

Research team
Claire Callender
South Bank University
103 Borough Road
London SE1 0AA
Tel: 020 7815 5729   Email: callencs@sbu.ac.uk\

Ros Edwards
South Bank University
Tel: 020 7818 5795   Email: edwardra@vax.sbu.ac.uk

Tracey Reynolds
South Bank University
Tel: 020 7815 5705   Email: reynoldta@sbu.ac.uk

Project summary

Mothers of young children account for a growing share of the labour force, and there is an increasing need for families to reconcile the demands of work with family life. Research on the topic rarely unpacks the aspects of working life that affect families. This study aimed to assess the impact of mothers' full- and part-time employment in two different service sector workplaces: a hospital and an accountancy firm. It examined the effects on the couple's material and emotional relationships, their parenting roles and relationships, their relationships with wider networks and sense of self. It was based on qualitative interviews with 37 mothers and 30 of their partners, interviewed separately, who had at least one child under 5 years old.

6 Balancing work and family lives in households where men or women enter self-employment from a position of disadvantage

Publications
Publication of Findings and report expected Autumn 2003.

Susan Baines, Jane Wheelock and Ulrike Gelder (forthcoming 2003) *Riding the rollercoaster: Family life and self-employment* (£13.95 tbc, ISBN 1 86134 503 8)

Research team
Susan Baines
University of Newcastle upon Tyne
Department of Sociology and Social Policy
Claremont Bridge Building
The University
Newcastle upon Tyne NE1 7RU
Tel: 0191 222 5031   Email: Susan.Baines@ncl.ac.uk

Jane Wheelock
University of Newcastle upon Tyne
Department of Sociology and Social Policy
Tel: 0191 222 7876   Email: Jane.Wheelock@ncl.ac.uk

Ulrike Gelder
University of Newcastle upon Tyne
Department of Sociology and Social Policy
Tel: 0191 222 7454   Email: I.U.Gelder@ucl.ac.uk

Project summary
Self-employment is promoted in government policy today, as it was two decades ago, under the banner of creating an 'entrepreneurial culture'. For people with a history of unemployment, limited skills and few resources, moving into self-employment is likely to involve low earnings and long working hours – factors known from other research to put pressure on families with children. Self-employed people cannot benefit from the family friendly policies of employing

organisations and may find that heavy and unpredictable workloads preclude the use of forms of childcare recognised by the National Childcare Strategy. There may, on the other hand, be more overlapping time for household members than is typical for many employed people. Little is known about how all this impacts on the ability of households reliant (in whole or in part) on self-employment to manage income earning and caring responsibilities.

The study location was the urban-rural fringe of the north east of England, where overall rates of self-employment are low and national and regional policies are directed at increasing them. At the heart of the methodology was a qualitative, household-based approach. Thirty households were recruited in order to address the complex, shifting nuances of family arrangements, working practices, and their co-ordination. Households were purposively selected from a database assembled for a quantitative study by the Centre for Rural Economy, University of Newcastle upon Tyne, and from other contacts. All households included at least one self-employed adult and one child under 12 years old. More than one adult was interviewed whenever applicable and possible. A selection of children and teenagers were interviewed, with the permission of their parents.

7 The impact of parental self-employment

Publications
Alice Bell and Ivana La Valle (June 2003) 'Combining self-employment and family life', Findings 663

Alice Bell and Ivana La Valle (2003) *Combining self-employment and family life* (£13.95 ISBN 1 86134 533 X)

Research team
Alice Bell
National Centre for Social Research
35 Northampton Square
London EC1V 0AX
Tel: 020 7549 9524   Email: a.bell@natcen.ac.uk

Ivana La Valle
National Centre for Social Research
Tel: 020 7549 9525 Email: i.lavalle@natcen.ac.uk

Project summary
Self-employment grew very rapidly in the 1980s and despite some signs of a slowdown in the latter part of the 1990s, it remains an important feature of the British labour market. There is some evidence that parents, and mothers in particular, might decide to enter self-employment because of the flexibility and autonomy one can have over the patterns and location of work. However, there is also some evidence that points to the potential negative impact self-employment could have on families, including long hours, poor pay and the financial insecurity associated with some forms of self-employment.

The study explored the work and family circumstances of self-employed parents and compared them with those of other working parents. More specifically, the study aimed to:

- Establish if and to what extent self-employed mothers and fathers are more likely to have 'atypical' work patterns.
- Compare the financial circumstances of self-employed parents with those of other working parents.
- Understand if and to what extent self-employed parents' influences on decisions to work differ from those of other working parents.
- Consider the use and availability of (affordable) childcare to meet the specific needs of self-employed parents.

The study carried out a secondary analysis of data from the DfES surveys of Parents' Demand for Childcare. Data from the two surveys was pooled, 1999 and 2001. In both cases, these cross-sectional surveys consisted of nationally representative samples of parents with a child under 14.

Employers' perspectives and the implementation of family-friendly employment policies

8 Nature and pattern of family friendly employment in Britain

Publications
Shirley Dex and Colin Smith (May 2002) 'The nature and pattern of family-friendly employment policies in Britain', Findings No. 5112

Shirley Dex and Colin Smith (2002) *The nature and pattern of family-friendly employment policies in Britain* (£12.95 ISBN 1 86134 433 3)

Research team
Shirley Dex
Centre for Longitudinal Studies
London University
20 Bedford Way
London WC1H 0AL
Email: sd@cls.ioe.ac.uk
(Formerly at University of Cambridge, Judge Institute of Management)

Colin Smith
Government Economic Service
London
(Formerly at University of Cambridge, Judge Institute of Management)

Sally Winter
(Formerly at Goldsmith's College, University of London)

Project summary

This research aimed to analyse three existing datasets which reveal the nature and patterns of family-friendly employment policy in Britain; these are the new Workplace Employee Relations Survey (WERS 98), the Department of Education and Employment's 1996 Family Friendly Working Arrangements Survey, and a 1998 survey of FTSE 100 companies. The WERS survey contained information on the extent of family-friendly working arrangements and has very rich data on other characteristics of the establishments as well as a valuable employee's perspective on the policies. The research examined the determinants of whether establishments have family-friendly policies, how many policies they have adopted, and their performance outcomes. Models of employee commitment were also constructed to see whether family-friendly policies influence levels of employee commitment. The models incorporated a range of explanatory variables which cover workplace characteristics and more structural market characteristics. In addition, some further analysis of two surveys of FTSE 100 companies examined the relationship between corporate responsibility agendas and family-friendly policies.

9 Firms' responses to the changing work–family arrangements

Publications

Shirley Dex and Fiona Scheibl (May 2002) 'Small organisations and flexible working arrangements', Findings No. 5102

Shirley Dex and Fiona Scheibl (2002) *SMEs and flexible working arrangements* (£12.95 ISBN 1 86134 432 5)

Research team
Shirley Dex
Centre for Longitudinal Studies
London University
20 Bedford Way
London WC1H 0AL
Email: sd@cls.ioe.ac.uk
(Formerly at University of Cambridge, Judge Institute of Management)

Fiona Scheibl
Health Services Research Unit
London School of Hygiene and Tropical Medicine
Keppel Street
London WC1E 7HT
(formerly at University of Cambridge, Judge Institute of Management)

Project summary

Earlier research on small and medium sized firms who have implemented flexible working arrangements has identified some of the reasons for their introduction and the business performance effects of these practices. In order to see whether these benefits could be transferred to other firms who do not have such arrangements, this research recruited and examined a set of matched case studies of small or medium sized employers who have not implemented any flexible or family-friendly working arrangements. Empirical work on the new case studies sought to investigate attitudes to flexible arrangements and the problems employers anticipate they would have if they were to implement any such arrangements. The study also compared employees' responses and needs in firms with and without family-friendly policies in order to identify what are genuinely family-friendly arrangements and good practice.

This project analysed 23 organisation case studies in the Eastern region (13 from this project and 10 from the early data collection). Qualitative research methods and interviews were carried out with employer representatives or owners of small businesses, general managers or human resource specialists and a selection of employees in each organisation.

10 Evaluating the effectiveness of support for working carers of older adults

Publications

Judith Phillips, Miriam Bernard and Minda Chittenden (July 2002) 'The experiences of working carers of older adults', Findings No. 7112

Judith Phillips, Miriam Bernard and Minda Chittenden (2002) *Juggling work and care: The experiences of working carers of older adults* (£10.95 ISBN 1 86134 443 0)

Research team
Judith Phillips
University of Keele
Centre for Social Gerontology
Keele
Staffordshire ST5 5BG
Tel: 01782 584067   Email: spa10@keele.ac.uk

Miriam Bernard
University of Keele
Centre for Social Gerontology
Tel: 01782 584063

Project summary
There has been no systematic research in Britain looking at the needs of working carers of older adults. The main aim of the research was to explore the use, relevance and effectiveness of a range of workplace policies and practices from the perspectives of

employers and carers in the public sector. To meet this aim, a questionnaire survey of employees in two large public sector settings (NHS and SSD) served to screen and recruit the employed carers of older adults who were sent a further questionnaire. These were accompanied by in depth interviews with carers and managers. The project highlighted good practice through reports, newsletters, articles and a conference.

A total of 2,431 employees responded to the initial postal screening survey; from this, 203 employees with caring responsibilities filled in a longer questionnaire.

11 Organisational decision-making and the provision of family-friendly policies

Publications
Sue Bond, Jeff Hyman, Juliette Summers and Sarah Wise (February 2002) 'Putting family-friendly working policies into practice', Findings No. 222

Sue Bond, Jeff Hyman, Juliette Summers and Sarah Wise (2002) *Family-friendly working? Putting policy into practice* (£14.95 ISBN 1 84263 050 4)

Research team
Jeff Hyman
Department of Management Studies
University of Aberdeen
Dunbar Street
Aberdeen AB24 3QY
Email: j.hyman@abdn.ac.uk
(Formerly at Glasgow Caledonian University, Department of Economics)

Sue Bond
Employment Research Institute
Napier University
Redwood House
66 Spylaw Road
Edinburgh EH10 5BR
Email: s.bond@napier.ac.uk

Juliette Summers
Department of Management and Organisation
Stirling University
Stirling FK9 4LA
Email: j.c.summers@stir.ac.uk
(Formerly at Employment Research Institute, Napier University)

Sarah Wise
Employment Research Institute
Napier University
Email: s.wise@napier.ac.uk

Poject summary

Drawing upon the prominent and generally progressive financial services sector in Scotland, this research aimed first to examine profiles of voluntary family friendly employment policies (FFPs) adopted by a sample of companies, their stated and effective coverage and their modes of operation. The second intention was to assess the ways in which employee participation can contribute to the establishment, maintenance, development and effectiveness of the policies and provision of benefits. With the broad political agenda in employment relations committed to voluntarism, social partnership and balance between work and family, the findings of the study will be of widespread public and policy interest. The research design consisted of two phases, commencing with an examination of definitions, procedures and structures for FFPs and employee participation in 17 finance sector organisations using postal survey methods. This phase was followed by in-depth studies of four organisations selected from the first stage. These case studies involved interviews, analysis of FFP provision and take-up, observation at meetings and surveys of staff and managers. The research commenced on 1 January 2000 and continued for a period of 14 months.

12 Employers, communities and family-friendly employment policies

Publications

Sue Yeandle, Rosemary Crompton, Andrea Wigfield and Jane Dennett (September 2002) 'Employers, communities and family-friendly employment policies', Findings No. 972

Sue Yeandle, Rosemary Crompton, Andrea Wigfield and Jane Dennett (2002) *Employed carers and family-friendly employment policies* (£11.95 ISBN 1 86134 480 5)

Research team
Sue Yeandle
Sheffield Hallam University
Centre for Regional Economic and Social Research
City Campus
Howard Street
Sheffield S1 1WB
Tel: 0114 225 2830 Email: s.m.yeandle@shu.ac.uk

Andrea Wigfield
University of Sheffield
Department of Sociological Studies
Elmfield

Northumberland Road
Sheffield S10 2TU
Tel: 0114 2224603 Email: a.wigfield@sheffield.ac.uk

Rosemary Crompton
City University
Department of Sociology
Northampton Square
London EC1V 0HB
Tel: 020 77040 8507 Email: r.crompton@city.ac.uk

Jane Dennett
Department of Social Policy
University of Kent
Canterbury CT2 7NY
Tel: 01227 827286 Email: J.Dennett@ukc.ac.uk
(Formerly at City University, Department of Sociology)

Project summary

The aims of the project were: to explore employment policies and practices affecting workers with caring responsibilities, with particular emphasis on care of the elderly; to assess whether there is scope for improving employers' links with the local infrastructure of care support; and to determine how far workers feel their caring responsibilities are recognised and supported by employers' policies and practices.

Case study methodology was used to explore experiences and practices in two contrasting locations (Sheffield and Canterbury) and in three employment sectors (banking and finance; retail; local authorities). To ensure that all relevant perceptions were identified, in each of the six case studies five data sources were used:

- semi-structured interviews with employers
- semi-structured interviews with trade unions or employees' representatives
- a questionnaire survey of employees
- focus groups with selected employees with caring responsibilities
- semi-structured interviews with service providers.

Workplace practices and work-family balance

13 Organisations, careers and caring

Publications

Publication of Findings and report expected Autumn 2003.

Rosemary Crompton, Jane Dennett and Andrea Wigfield (forthcoming 2003) *Organisations, careers and caring* (£11.95 tbc, ISBN 1 86134 500 3)

Research team
Rosemary Crompton
City University
Department of Sociology
Northampton Square
London EC1V 0HB
Tel: 020 7040 8507 Email: R.Crompton@city.ac.uk

Jane Dennett
Department of Social Policy
University of Kent
Canterbury CT2 7NY
Tel: 01227 827286 Email: J.Dennett@ukc.ac.uk
(Formerly at City University, Department of Sociology)

Andrea Wigfield
University of Sheffield
Department of Sociological Studies
Elmfield
Northumberland Road
Sheffield S10 2TU
Tel 0114 2224603 Email: a.wigfield@sheffield.ac.uk

Project summary
Until the 1980s, men who engaged in long-term careers could usually rely on the support of a non-working wife. However, women have increasingly been gaining qualifications and moving into higher-level occupations, and such women tend to enter into partnerships with similar men.

Thus the tensions between paid employment and caring responsibilities have increasingly been recognised. In Britain, these changes have been reflected in recent policy statements, and more employers are offering 'family-friendly' policies to their employees. In parallel with these policy developments, the processes of organisational restructuring have generated increases in flexible working and flatter organisational hierarchies, which should, in theory, improve the possibilities for individuals wishing to pursue a 'flexible career'.

This project investigated, through a comparative analysis of matched biographies, what happens to the promotion and career prospects of those who take up offers of flexible work, compared with those who do not. It also explored men's attitudes to, and the implementation of, carer-friendly employment practices. The research was carried out in two localities (Canterbury and Sheffield) and in three employment sectors (banking, local government, and retail) - building on contacts made during the course of fieldwork for the study described at project 12 above.

14 The dynamics of the family–work interface among ethnic minority businesses in Britain

Publications
Publication of Findings and report expected Autumn 2003.

Anuradha Basu and Eser Altinay (forthcoming 2003) *Family and work in ethnic minority businesses* (£11.95 tbc, ISBN 1 86134 548 8)

Research team
Anuradha Basu
University of Reading
School of Business
Department of Management
PO Box 218
Whiteknights
Reading RG6 6AA
Tel: 0118 987 5123 ext. 4344 Email: a.basu@reading.ac.uk

Eser Altinay
University of Reading
Email: e.altinay@reading.ac.uk

Project summary
This research project focused on the changing nature of the family-work overlap with business growth, a neglected area of research. It did so in the context of ethnic minority businesses and investigated the effects of running a family business alongside organising family life for a range of ethnic minority groups in Britain.

The study examined the nature of the family's involvement in business and its effects on family lives, as well as the diversity among family-owned ethnic minority businesses with respect to their views on the family-work interface and the role of family in business. The research highlighted the dynamic nature of the family-work interface over time, in line with stages in the business cycle from business start-up to maturity and, alongside this, stages in the family cycle.

These issues were examined on the basis of face-to-face interviews with 60 ethnic minority entrepreneurs in the South East of England, and 17 of their wives. The entrepreneurs come from five ethnic groups (Bangladeshi, East African Asian, Indian, Pakistani and Turkish-Cypriot), approximately 12 in each. They were interviewed about their family's involvement in the business at business start-up and at the time of the interviews and the effects of that involvement on family life.

15 Family-friendly working arrangements: attitudes and uptake in men and women

Publications
Publication of Findings and report expected Autumn 2003.

Diane M. Houston and Julie A. Waumsley (forthcoming, 2003) *Attitudes to flexible working and family life* (£13.95 tbc, ISBN 1 86134 549 6)

Research team
Diane Houston
University of Kent at Canterbury
Department of Psychology
Keynes College
Canterbury CT2 7NP
Tel: 01227 827933 Email: d.m.houston@ukc.ac.uk

Julie Waumsley
University of Kent at Canterbury
Department of Psychology
Tel: 01227 823923 Email: j.a.waumsley@ukc.ac.uk

Project summary
The overall aim of the research was to examine and compare attitudes to, and uptake of, family-friendly work practices by women and men. The research also examined the ways in which workplace culture and individual circumstances determine responses to family-friendly practices. Perceptions of the career implications of family-friendly working were also explored.

A questionnaire survey of 1,500 male and female managerial, skilled and semi-skilled workers was conducted through the Amalgamated Engineering and Electrical Union (now merged with MSF to become AMICUS). The questionnaire focused on the types of family-friendly practices available to workers, attitudes towards these and their uptake. Data analysis provided comparisons between men and women, managerial, skilled and semi-skilled workers, and those with and without current caring responsibilities.

In the second year of the project, semi-structured interviews with 40 shop stewards, who are trained to negotiate between workers and management, provided a unique insight into perceptions of family-friendly policies. These interviews examined issues raised by the questionnaire data.

16 Geographical mobility: Family impacts

Publications
Anne E. Green and Angela Canny (May 2003) 'The effects on families of job relocations', Findings No. 533

Anne E. Green and Angela Canny (2003) *Geographical mobility: Family impacts* (£13.95 ISBN
1 86134 501 1)

Research team
Anne E. Green
University of Warwick
Institute for Employment Research
Coventry CV4 7AL
Tel: 024 7652 4113 Email: A.E.Green@warwick.ac.uk

Angela Canny
Mary Immaculate College
University of Limerick
Department of Education
South Circular Road
Limerick
Ireland
Tel: 00 353 61 204598   Email: Angela.Canny@mic.ul.ie
(Formerly at University of Warwick, Institute for Employment Research)

Project summary
Some employers have a need to move staff between locations for career progression
purposes and to meet skills needs. While the initial emphasis of formal relocation policies
was on financial support for employees undertaking moves, there is increasing recognition
that geographical mobility poses challenges for family life. Relocatees are often concerned
about practical support in family-related matters – including schooling and partner's
employment.

This project aimed to:

- chart the changing role and nature of geographical mobility, especially relocation, in
  career development and corporate strategies
- investigate the working and family life experiences of relocatees
- explore family member experiences of geographical mobility
- assess the consequences of geographical mobility on career development
- identify good practice in geographical mobility policies that help to reduce 'family
  frictions' associated with mobility.

The project explored corporate and individual views on the experience of geographical
mobility. It involved: limited background secondary data analysis; interviews with key
players; employer interviews; interviews with 30 employees who have relocated; and
interviews with partners of employees.

Implications for family life and childcare of flexible working arrangements

17 Parents' atypical work patterns and impact on family life

Publications

Ivana La Valle, Sue Arthur, Christine Millward, James Scott and Marion Clayden (September 2002) 'The influence of atypical working hours on family life', Findings No. 982

Ivana La Valle, Sue Arthur, Christine Millward, James Scott with Marion Clayden (2002) *Happy families? Atypical work and its influence on family life* (£14.95 ISBN 1 86134 481 3)

Research team
Ivana La Valle
National Centre for Social Research
35 Northampton Square
London EC1V 0AX
Tel: 020 7549 9525 Email: i.lavalle@natcen.ac.uk

Sue Arthur
National Centre for Social Research
Tel: 020 7549 9543 Email: s.arthur@natcen.ac.uk

Project summary
Ongoing changes in corporate work practices and technologies, the globalisation of the economy and the move towards the '24-hour society' have led to an increase in what are broadly termed 'atypical' work patterns (such as weekend and shift working). There is already some evidence that the increase in 'unsocial' working hours results in less 'overlapping' time that parents and children can spend together. This study investigated further what impact parents' atypical work patterns have on the quantity and quality of 'overlapping' family time, and the reasons behind parents' atypical work patterns. The study included three stages:

- Further analysis of relevant data from the survey of Parents' Demand for Childcare (a baseline survey which measured parental use of and demand for childcare, conducted by the National Centre in 1999 on behalf of the Department for Education and Employment).
- A quantitative telephone follow-up survey of parents from the survey of Parents' Demand for Childcare. The follow-up survey enabled measurement of the prevalence of different forms of atypical working hours and their associations with childcare use, parenting roles and family activities.
- Qualitative research comprising 40 in-depth interviews with purposively selected respondents to give a more detailed understanding of the circumstances of parents working atypical hours and the impact on their family life.

18 Managing childcare needs and flexible work arrangements

Publications
Christine Skinner (May 2003) 'How parents co-ordinate childcare, education, and work',
Findings No. 593

Christine Skinner (2003) *Running around in circles: Co-ordinating childcare, education and work* (£14.95 ISBN 1 86134 466 X)

Research team
Christine Skinner
University of York
Department of Social Policy and Social Work
Heslington
York YO10 5DD
Tel: 01904 434723 Email: cbes100@york.ac.uk

Project summary
The government's National Childcare Strategy aims to improve childcare services across the UK. While some improvements have been made, parents still face the complex task of co-ordinating educational and childcare services to meet the needs of all the children in the family. The process of co-ordinating the times of different childcare provision with work commitments, and the logistics of travelling between childcare and educational services, the home and the workplace are not trivial barriers to women's access to paid work. The aim of this study was to explore the ways in which parents in two specific localities in the same city (20 in each) manage the interface between an array of childcare/educational services and work commitments. The difficulties of managing this interface and the resultant potential barriers posed to employment and to reconciling work and family life were considered. The study exploited existing qualitative interview data collected in England in the late 1990s as part of a wider European project. The focus of this study is central to current debates about the work participation rates of mothers, the difficulties of balancing work and family life and the aim of policy to improve childcare services.

19 Childcare services and atypical working hours

Publications
June Statham and Ann Mooney (2003) *Around the clock: Childcare services at atypical times* (£11.95 ISBN 1 86134 502 X)

Research team
Ann Mooney
Thomas Coram Research Unit
Institute of Education
27/28 Woburn Square

London WC1H 0AA
Tel: 0207 612 6948 Email: tetcaam@ioe.ac.uk.

June Statham
Thomas Coram Research Unit
Tel: 01686 629624 Email: j.statham@ioe.ac.uk

Project summary

The provision of good quality childcare services is an important factor within government strategies to reconcile work and family life, and to reduce child poverty and social exclusion. Since the launch of the National Childcare Strategy in May 1998, there has been a rapid expansion of childcare provision, with further expansion planned. However, there is little information as to whether this provision meets the needs of a growing number of employees who require childcare outside regular working hours. The growth of a '24-hour society' has meant that more people are now working outside the 'standard' 9 to 5 day. Increasing numbers of employers depend upon round the clock availability of their workers, often at short notice or on unpredictable shift patterns. People in professional and managerial positions may be compensated for working long or unsociable hours by high salaries. However, shift work and jobs that involve irregular hours are usually linked to low pay and high levels of job insecurity. Finding childcare that is both affordable and available for the hours needed may therefore be problematical. This nine-month study examined the factors that prevent childcare providers offering a service that covers atypical hours.

A survey of Early Years Development and Childcare Partnerships provided information on barriers and incidences of services at a national level and telephone interviews were conducted with key officers of national organisations representing the childcare industry. A sample of different types of formal childcare providers in each of two contrasting authorities were then surveyed to elicit information on their willingness to offer childcare for atypical hours and the factors that would facilitate or hinder them from offering such a service. Six case studies of childcare providers who did offer a service to meet the needs of employees working non-standard hours were conducted and focused on: how the service was set up, any difficulties faced and how they were resolved, response from parents and lessons for future practice.

20 Line managers' roles

Publications
Publication of Findings and report expected Winter 2003.

Sue Yeandle, Judith Phillips, Fiona Scheibl, Andrea Wigfield, and Sarah Wise (forthcoming 2003) *Line managers' roles in implementing family-friendly employment* (£11.95 tbc ISBN 1 86134 556 9)

Research team

Sue Yeandle
Sheffield Hallam University
Centre for Regional Economic and Social Research
City Campus
Howard Street
Sheffield S1 1WB
Tel: 0114 225 2830   Email: s.m.yeandle@shu.ac.uk

Judith Phillips
University of Keele
Centre for Social Gerontology
Keele
Staffordshire ST5 5BG
Tel: 01782 584067   Email: spa10@keele.ac.uk

Fiona Scheibl
Health Services Research Unit
London School of Hygiene and Tropical Medicine
Kepple Street
London WC1E 7HT
(Formerly at the University of Cambridge, Judge Institute of Management)

Andrea Wigfield
University of Sheffield
Department of Sociological Studies
Elmfield
Northumberland Road
Sheffield S10 2TU
Tel: 0114 222460   Email: a.wigfield@sheffield.ac.uk
(Formerly at Sheffield Hallam University)

Sarah Wise
Employment Research Institute
Napier University
Redwood House
66 Spylaw Road
Edinburgh EH10 5BR
Email: s.wise@napier.ac.uk

Project summary
This project carried out secondary analysis of interviews with line managers, other managers and some employees collected in four earlier projects from the Work and Family Life Programme (projects 9, 10, 11 and 12 above). While each of the four initial projects contained only a few interviews with line managers, pooling the data from these different sources was seen as an opportunity to explore line managers' roles across a range of settings

– including differences in sizes of organisation, industry sector, public/private sectors, types of work, workplace arrangements and working practices. In addition, differences in attitudes and experience of line managers could be explored, including their own experiences of caring. The organisations providing interviews included financial services organisations in Scotland, an NHS Trust and social services department, small and medium sized businesses across manufacturing, services and high-tech companies in East Anglia, two branches of a retail bank and a major supermarket, and two local councils. Pooling these interviews meant that over 80 interviews with line managers were available for secondary analysis. Researchers from the four original research teams participated in the project and together drew up a framework, issues and themes for the analysis. These researchers then supplied to a coordinator, material from their original interviews relevant to the themes identified. The coordinator analysed and collated this material and an iterative process enabled individual researchers to check and comment on the new analyses and the written document.

The project shows how line managers, their experiences, values and job tenure, along with the staffing policies in organisations, all play a crucial role in interpreting and defining organisations' policies and practices. Some recommendations for improvement and better practice implementation of flexible working arrangements are drawn out of the findings.

Funded outside the Work and Family Life research programme

1 Children with disabilities – guidebook and support for parents

Publications
Sarah Litvinoff, Janet Mearns and Sue Monk (1999) *Waving not drowning: A guide for parents trying to combine paid work and caring for disabled children* (£2.99 parents; £11.99 single copy/funded organisations). Published by Parents at Work and available from www.parentsatwork.org.uk

Contact
Parents at Work
Fifth Floor, 45 Beech Street
London EC2
Tel: 0207 628 3578

Project summary
Barriers to work for parents of disabled children are substantial, with disproportionate levels of unemployment. This project addressed the employment-related support needs of parents of disabled children in a practical way through the production of a newsletter, a parents' contact directory, and a helpline. The guidebook gathers together in one place essential information and practical advice for parents who are working or who want to work.

2 Review of Families and Work

Publications

Shirley Dex (Editor) with contributions by Louie Burghes, Lynda Clarke, Shirley Dex, Sally Holtermann, Marion Kozak, Francis McGlone, Juliet Mountford, Ceridwen Roberts and Fiona Scheibl (1999) *Families and the labour market: Trends, pressures and policies.* Published by FPSC/JRF. Out of print.

Contact
Ceridwen Roberts
Department of Social Policy and Social Work
University of Oxford
Barnett House
32 Wellington Square
Oxford OX1 2ER
Email: ceridwen.roberts@socres.ox.ac.uk
(Formerly at Family Policy Studies Centre)

Project summary

This review is seen as a successor to the 1982 publication *Employment trends and the family* (Study Centre on the Family), with a focus on the 15 years since the publication of that report. This publication is in three parts. Part I (Setting the Scene) covers social and family change and labour market change. Part II (Families and Work) covers the relationships between employment and changes in marriage, parenthood and caring responsibilities. Part III (The consequences for family life) examines the financial, economic and health and well-being consequences of employment for family life. The final section, Part IV (Supporting families at work and getting the balance right), discusses changes in public provision and employer practices and policy implications relevant to these issues.

3 Fathers, work and family life: The construction of paternal roles in families with teenagers

Publications

Jo Warin and Charlie Lewis (June 1999) 'Fathers, work and family life', Findings No. 659

Jo Warin and Charlie Lewis (1999) *Fathers, work and family life* (£10.95
ISBN 1 901455 36 X). Published by FPSC/JRF. Available from JRF (www.jrf.org.uk).

Charlie Lewis (April 2000) 'A man's place in the home: Fathers and families in the UK', Foundations No. 440. Available from JRF (www.jrf.org.uk).

Contact
Charlie Lewis
University of Lancaster
Department of Psychology

Bailrigg

Lancaster LA1 4YF

Tel: 01524 65201 Email: c.lewis@lancaster.ac.uk

Project summary

The main aims of this research were to gain knowledge about the part played by fathers in families with a secondary-school aged child and to consider paternal involvement in the light of both parents' involvement in the labour market over the course of the child's life. A follow-up survey of a sample of 180 families studied in 1987 provided data concerning parental employment and parental involvement in the home. Follow-up interviews explored the father's, the mother's and the child(ren)'s understanding of fatherhood in contemporary families.

Work and Opportunity programme

The JRF Work and Opportunity research programme which ran in parallel with the Work and Family Life programme contributed a number of projects that were relevant to WFL priorities. Reports are published in the Work and Opportunity series and are available from York Publishing Services Ltd (Tel: 01904 430033) or via the JRF website (www.jrf.org.uk).

Background to Work and Family Life research programme

As well as two seminars held in 1996 and 1997, a number of projects previously supported by JRF have directly informed thinking about this programme.

These include:

Peter Clarke, Cheri Viniall and others (1998) *Raising the standard: The code of practice for children's information service.* Published by Choices in Childcare. Out of print.

Carolyn Kagan, Suzan Lewis and Patricia Heaton (May 1998) 'Combining work and care: Working parents of disabled children' Findings No. 538

Louie Burghes, Lynda Clarke and Natalie Cronin (July 1997) 'Fathers and fatherhood in Britain', Findings No. SP120

Elsa Ferri and Kate Smith (October 1996) 'Parenting in the 1990s', Findings No. SP106

Exploring parenthood (January 1995) 'Developing work and family services in the workplace', Findings No. SP69